BEYOND THE BLACK PIG'S DYKE

A SHORT HISTORY OF ULSTER

ART Ó BROIN

MERCIER PRESS

Mercier Press
PO Box 5 5 French Church Street Cork
16 Hume Street Dublin 2

First published 1995

A CIP record for this book is available from the British Library.

ISBN 1 85635 114 9

10 9 8 7 6 5 4 3 2 1

Cover painting: View of West Bank Quays City of Derry 1846 by John Noah Gosset © Derry City Council
Cover design by Bluett
Typeset by Richard Parfrey
Printed in Ireland by ColourBooks Baldoyle Dublin 13

CONTENTS

. . . and the great black boar, driven mad in its bewitchment, dug with its tusks a long straight deep ditch that has ever since been known as the Black Pig's Dyke.

ACROSS THE NARROW SEA
THE LAND AND ITS FIRST PEOPLE

The shape of Ireland is a product of the most recent Ice Age which had more or less spent itself by 11,000 BC. Its particular legacy to Ulster were the smooth-scraped U-valleys in central Donegal and the Mourne mountains of southeast Down, and the pimpling of drumlins that stretches from the loughs of Strangford and Carlingford in a wide swathe through Monaghan, Cavan and south Tyrone as far west as Donegal Bay.

With the thaw and the slow drying-out of the land of northern Europe came vegetation, animals for hunting and hunters to follow them. The rise of water levels caused by the melting of nearly 100,000 years of ice eventually formed the southern North Sea and covered the land bridges that had linked these western fringes with the continent of Europe. The northeast of Antrim was connected to modern Strathclyde; every Irish child knows why the basalt formations of the Giant's Causeway look very like those in Fingal's Cave in Staffa. There is evidence of a broader land connection in that the Derryveagh mountains of Donegal are geologically kin to the Sperrins in Derry and Tyrone, and to the Cairngorms in the central highlands of Scotland.

The first inhabitants could have come over by the same tracks that brought the great elk. Even now a mere thirteen miles separates Scotland and Ulster at their closest and in the mesolithic period, when it is known that there was habitation and settlement in Ireland, the land masses of Ireland and Britain were considerably closer together. Since present-day Scotland and Ireland are each clearly visible from the other it has long been assumed that the aboriginal Ulstermen came by a short sea-route from the Mull of Kintyre to Fair Head or from Dumfries to Larne, or even from Islay to Inishowen, if not on foot then in skin curraghs or dug-out canoes. Yet the findings of recent scholarship, based on comparison of artefacts, suggest that the first wanderers landed in Down near Carlingford Lough or perhaps as far south as Wicklow. At this time the British mainland extended considerably to the west of the Isle of Man. Once landed they would have moved north and southwest. This would explain why excavations at places as far apart as Mount Sandel near Coleraine and Lough Boora near Tullamore show evidence of contemporaneous human settlement around 8,000 BC.

The terrain that these neolithic hunters found was a naturally distinct part of the post Ice-Age island. The drumlin barrier, referred to with increasingly fanciful degrees of imagery by successive academics at the Queen's University of Belfast as a basket of eggs and a necklace of beads, tended to cut off Ulster from the rest of the country. These small lopsided hills had generally impassable patches of bog and wetland between them and in time the barrier effect was increased by the earthwork known as the Black Pig's Dyke. Remains of this Hadrian's Wall in reverse, originally built

6

to block places where the drumlin belt left gaps, may still be seen in south Donegal and Monaghan. A section called the Dorsey in south Armagh must have been regarded as an approved crossing-place since the name comes from the Gaelic *doirse* (=doors).

The combination of nature and man remained extremely effective. The dyke served to cut off the northern territory from the rest of the island right to the end of the sixteenth century. In the Nine Years' War between Hugh O'Neill and his Tudor adversaries there were only two relatively easy ways into Ulster, by the Moyry Pass in County Armagh and by the Erne waters in the west. Much has been made of Ulster's separateness, largely for propaganda purposes in the last hundred years, but just as the Shannon is accepted as an approximate natural boundary for Connacht, so the Black Pig's Dyke acted both metaphorically and literally to preserve the northern terrain from influences and changes – and dangers – that affected the rest of Ireland.

By historical times the territory thus demarked had developed characteristics not shared by the rest of the country. It was an Ireland in miniature in that there was fertile lowland to the east and south and poorer hillier land elsewhere. The river Bann, flowing from the Mournes into the huge Lough Neagh (by these islands' standards an inner sea) and emerging again to run by Lough Beg to the sea at Coleraine, neatly divided the area in two. (It was to act as a political and moral line of division nearly 10,000 years later.) In the west the river Foyle in its avatars, Mourne and Strule and with its tributaries, Finn and Derg, was to be a kind of northern Shannon offering navigable waterways deep into modern Tyrone and Donegal and with easy land-journeys to the Erne in Fermanagh and the Blackwater in Armagh. Belfast Lough and the Lagan gave a way into east Down while the Ards peninsula and Strangford, like Lough Foyle and Lough Swilly in the northwest, provided both access to and haven from the often stormy seas.

Except for the higher peaks the country was thickly wooded, where it was not boggy, with oak, alder and elm the predominant species. The rivers were famous for the abundance of fish, especially the spawning salmon, and with the mild moist climate, grass was rich and plentiful. The farmers tended to favour cattle rather than cultivation and since their herds could graze in summer on quite high ground the people could survive bad crop seasons and the famines induced by the Tudor captains by taking to this higher ground and denser forest. The Antrim plateau, mainly basalt with ribs of nine glens running down to the North Channel, was fairly trackless but since settlements were generally coastal, journeys when undertaken were most conveniently made by sea. Offshore islands like Tory and Aranmore in Donegal and Rathlin north of Fair Head in Antrim were not regarded as particularly inaccessible. For if Ulster was cordoned off by its drumlin force-field it was open to Scotland, and Antrim, part of the later kingdom of Dál Riata, was as Scots as it was Irish. Journeys to the west coast of Alba were considerably easier and quicker than to Leinster. And the Romans saw no difference between the people who lived on different sides of the North Channel:

both were to them *Scoti*. (The name once gave rise to a gibe by a king and a sharp riposte by an Irish philosopher. Charles the Bald, the ninth-century King of France, once at table teased his mentor Johannes Scotus Eriugena, the Irish *doctus*, by asking tipsily in Latin: 'What is the difference between an Irishman (*Scotus*) and a drunkard (*sottus*)?' 'The width of this table,' came the Irish answer.)

The psychological and sociological effects of this separateness continued to affect what became known as the province of Ulster throughout its history. It was not 'Normanised' to the same extent as Leinster and it retained its Gaelic culture later than the other provinces. This virtual autonomy rendered it very conservative but did not preclude continual internecine struggles between rival chieftains. In time it provided Scotland with its religion and language. Even in modern times the Irish of Rathlin and Donegal showed significant links with Scots Gaelic. And its final colonisation was effected mainly by Scots, most obviously at the time of the Ulster plantation but also, because of an unchallenged assumption that the North Channel was not a national boundary, before and after the formal parcelling. In a sense the territories that became Antrim and Down were Scottish, and Argyll, Dumfries and Galloway and the Inner Hebrides at least partly Irish.

The first Ulstermen were hunters and fishers and tended to settle, however temporarily, by lakes, rivers and seashores. The Mount Sandel excavations showed evidence of a diet of seafood, fresh fruit, hazel nuts, beef (from wild cattle), venison and game. Axes, harpoons (for spearing fish), arrows and knives of flint and porcellanite were used by these early inhabitants. They seem to have come in small bands of, say, a hundred people and constituted the first of many tides of immigration to the wintry island that the unconquering Romans later called *Hibernia*. For a period of nearly a thousand years, from approximately 7,000 to 6,000BC, there is no archaeological evidence of any further immigration. The Irish Sea grew wider, and the narrow Stranraer-Larne passage may very well have been the route of entry for some later Ulstermen.

The people of this next wave were farmers rather than hunters. Neolithic man no longer needed to depend on the killing of animals for survival. He had learnt to control his environment and could grow grain, tame non-predatory wild animals and develop the ox and cow as work beasts and food providers, and use sheep and goats for clothing and cheeses. This revolutionary (or evolutionary?) change began sometime in the fifth millennium BC when pressure of population in the eastern Mediterranean caused an exodus north and west through the Balkans and across northern Europe. These agriculturists probably reached Ireland about the middle of the fourth millennium. They still tended to settle in clearings or by river banks or by lakes and the sea's edge. The clearings were sometimes made by felling trees but ringbarking proved much more rapid a method of arboreal destruction. There was plenty of timber for the building of dwellings and protective stockades against wolf, bear, lynx and fox, and the inevitable human enemies. Pottery was fired in timber kilns and skins were prepared for raiment with flint- or porcellanite-headed scrapers. The reconstruction of a neolithic house excavated near Cookstown shows it to have been rectangular in shape with oak posts both inside and out to hold up the walls and the thatched roof, which was pitched to allow the frequent rains to run off. There was a central hearth but no chimney. Carbon dating suggests that the house was destroyed by fire around 3,700BC.

There was, too, among these skilful people some sense of religion and of the mystery of death. They were probably ancestor worshippers and stored the ashes of their dead in megalithic court cairns which doubled as primitive shrines. The dead were also buried in dolmens, those impressive examples of primitive engineering consisting of huge upright boulders topped by a roofstone. It was about this period that the great passage-tombs at Newgrange, Knowth and Dowth in the Boyne valley were constructed, but perhaps because of the drumlin barrier the Ulster folk were not much influenced by that level of mathematical and aesthetic achievement.

The Bronze Age, which began sometime around 2000BC, showed a further technological advance: metalwork began to be a part of the life of the people. It was also characterised by a change in burial arrangements which in turn indicates a greater awareness of individuality. Corpses were buried in single graves and, as food utensils for the immortal spirits, ornamented cups designated by archaeologists as 'beakers' were placed beside the bodies. The age saw the forging of copper and tin weapons and the making of gold ornaments of which the *lunulae* (=small moons) are the best known and taken to be most characteristic of the period by the non-specialist. This was the time when Ireland began to develop its reputation as an important exporter of copper and gold products. The level of sophistication of these works of art shows them to be products of a genuine if early civilisation. But as often in the prehistory of Ireland there are great gaps in evidence. Lacunae are more characteristic than coherence. What is certain is that the coming of the Iron Age showed a deterioration of weather conditions resulting in an increase in the number of lowland settlements, and the making of a greater number of war weapons. By the middle of the last millennium BC a new folk immigration had occurred and these men and women were to be characterised by sentiment-al, hungry-for-heroes nineteenth-century poets as the Irish equivalent of the Homeric warriors of the Aegean.

– 2 –

'TALLER THAN ROMAN SPEARS'
THE CELTS

The history of Ireland, certainly since the middle of the sixteenth century, gave the nineteenth-century Irish very little to exult about. There had been heroism aplenty but little success, and any gains seemed so quickly to have been dissipated by political incompetence, bloody-mindedness and greed. The one perfect period, it seemed, in the distressful country's story, was that of the Celts, and Thomas D'Arcy McGee's poem summed up the pride and the relief with which they were regarded by his countrymen as they began the slow climb to nationhood again:

> Long, long ago, beyond the mighty space
> Of twice a thousand years,
> In Erin old there dwelt a mighty race,
> Taller than Roman spears . . .

It was a sentimentalised, romantic picture and yet as far as their vernacular literature was concerned it was true that, 'Great were their deeds, their passions and their sports.' It is in their literature that McGee's warriors live. This was preserved in the twelfth-century manuscripts the *Book of the Dun Cow* and *Book of Leinster* and the fourteenth-century *Yellow Book of Lecan*. The stories of hard-riding and chariot-

13

driving warriors and their remarkably independent women were not written down until then but there is no doubt about their antiquity, which dates from the first centuries AD. They were preserved orally by the *filid*, the class of intellectual poet-chroniclers who learnt the wisdom of the race and were responsible for its safe transmission. The tales were told mainly in prose with highlights in verse and though there were inevitable modifications as the centuries passed, even in the language used, as Primitive Irish became Old Irish, the lore on the whole reflected the conservatism of the class. Their jealously preserved mystery included the memorising of all known knowledge about the Celtic past. There was a tradition that a sixth-century king of Ulster, Mongan, the son of Fiachna, was entertained with a different story from the tradition by Forgall, his *file*, every night from *Samhain* to *Bealtaine*.

The lore inevitably mixed history with epic stories and it is the job of the archaeologist to separate the one from the other. The famous *Táin Bó Cuailgne*, which tells a wonder tale of a struggle between the men of Connacht under their queen Medb and the heroes of Ulster led by Cú Chulainn, may contain some memory of an actual battle which expelled the men of Ulaid from the western part and drove them beyond the Bann. The *Lebor Gabála* (The Book of Invasions) with its sequence of invaders, Partholón, Nemed mac Agnomain, the Fomorians, the Fir Bolg, the Tuatha Dé Danann and finally the Milesians, was no doubt generated from memories of different waves of Celtic and pre-Celtic immigration into Munster and Ulster. (The Fir

Bolg are thought to have been the Belgae though the name has connotations of dwarfishness (*bolg*=belly) and may be a comment on the difference in height between the tall warrior class and the smaller opposition.) The battles, court life and games detailed in these epics match what is known of Celtic life in Europe at its zenith and is not all that far removed from Homer's Aegean.

These people, who originated in central Europe and were known to the Greeks as *Keltoi*, had a common language (the remote ancestor of modern Irish), an eccentric and very complicated system of reckoning kinship, a taste for storytelling and a way with horses. They effortlessly subdued the existing inhabitants because of their chariot mobility, superior weapons and battle tactics but their assumption of the lordship of the various parts of their new country would have been gradual, extending, some authorities say, over as many as 1,500 years. And there is no reason to consider their hegemony that of an army of occupation or to assume that their mastery was achieved by extreme militarism. Perhaps their accommodation with people from previous waves of immigration was that of positive assimilation.

The continental Celts had been a dominant race in northern Europe, successfully harrying Rome and the Greek islands, establishing settlements in Asia Minor and Spain. Their language was kin to Latin and they brought their gods with them. The sun god, Lugh, gave names to things as various as the capital city of England and the Irish word for August. Their most characteristic form of decoration, which they engraved on pillar-stones and burial mounds, and with which they embellished their pottery, jewellry and metalwork, is called *La Tène*, from a site in Switzerland which gave its name to the Celtic culture of the late Iron Age. They settled most firmly in Britain and modern France which the Romans called Gaul and their coming to Ireland was undertaken at many different times and from different ports of embarkation. Their *ur*-language suffered a semantic change and philologists distinguish between *p*-Celtic and *q*-Celtic, the one evolving into Welsh, Breton and Kernow, the second producing Irish, Manx and Gaelic. The *Pritani* became the Picts of Scotland and settled in East Ulster as *Cruithni*.

It is likely that the Ulster Celts came from Britain by the now wider and deeper North Channel but by historical times (c. AD 500) the pattern of life throughout the island had reached a formality and consistency that was to last till the end of the sixteenth century. The coming of Christianity, the inroads and commercial settlements of the Vikings and the establishment of the Norman Pale were, of course, to modify but not ultimately to change the antique, subtle and Byzantinely complicated societal patterns of these extra-ordinary people.

As a simplification of the complexity of the system we may note that primogeniture, the usual basis for inheritance, was not especially significant. The Irish ruling class regarded themselves as belonging to a family group called a *fine*. The scheme was drawn up by the brehons, the law-makers, and concerned the relationship between a man and his brothers.

This unity was extended over five generations and it was both defensive and sanctional. The group administered laws internally, taking responsibility for crimes committed by the members and exacting punishment for crimes done against them. The greatest duty was of blood-vengeance against the killer of a member, though often an *éraic* (payment) was accepted in lieu. It follows that *fingal*, the slaying of a kinsman, was regarded as the unforgivable and uncompensatable crime.

The country as a whole was divided into a number of petty kingdoms called *tuatha*, each with a king at its head. The king was known as the *rí* and in the royal *fine* each member was regarded as a possible heir. To prevent monopolisation of the monarchy by a particular branch of the *fine* often a *tánaise ríg* or heir apparent was elected during the *rí's* lifetime. (Women could not succeed to land-title, though daughters without brothers could hold a life interest in their father's land.) Though the monarchical system lapsed after the Norman invasion, the *fine* still persisted and it was not very clear to outsiders who would succeed as clan chief in the ruling families. The Tudors, used to the idea of primogeniture and not subscribing to the Salic Law, found the Gaelic system dense to incomprehensible. It did not suit their peacetime policy of containing a wayward chief during his lifetime, while training the heir as they wished him to develop. This was the main stimulus to the 'surrender and regrant' scheme by which they hoped to change the character of Gaelic Ulster.

Within each *tuath* there were well-defined strata of society under the *rí*. Wealth was as important as birth, and in a society without money wealth consisted of land, beasts and slaves. These latter two were used as units of exchange. The *áes dána*, or learned class of brehons, poets, chroniclers, had very high status and since the system was preserved up until the early seventeenth century the poets felt the change of fortune as severely as the chiefs and reacted vocally and plaintively. All freemen were allotted land and franchise was earnable by a subject's becoming a skilled craftsman. Smiths, physicians, harpers, armourers, masons and the rest were freemen, the word for 'artificer' and the word for 'free' having the same root. The unfree classes included serfs, labourers and entertainers.

Though the Celts in Europe and Britain had the epic reputation of warriors and were noted for their hilltop strongholds, by the coming of Christianity the Irish Celts, royal and base, were farmers and their characteristic dwellings raths and crannogs. The use of the rath (*ráth*=earthen rampart) was universal and many have survived as 'fairy forts'. These, sometimes with double or triple mounds and ditches, enclosed an area with a house, square or round, and outbuildings. The earthworks acted as defences, corrals and boundaries. Souterrains were often constructed near the raths and their purpose, like the round towers of later centuries, was mainly as places of refuge, though the outer chambers were used as stores. The crannogs (*crannóg*=wooden frame) were artificial islands created by setting up a ring of timber piles in the middle of a shallow lake and filling in the space with brushwood, stone and earth. They were about thirty metres in diameter and accessible only by boat or underwater causeway. They were what modern estate-agents would call desirable residences and probably owned by the most aristocratic members of the *tuath*. Their defensive properties are clear and they may have been prized for their location and their appearance.

With over a hundred *tuatha* in the island and no central government as we understand the word, the likelihood of tribal wars was strong. It is hard to separate myth from fact, epic hero from actual leader. Not long after the beginning of the fifth century a semi-historical figure, Niall Noígiallach ('Niall of the nine hostages'), appears. He was of Connacht and is taken to be the founder of the Uí Néill, who weakened the power of the Ulaid and drove them into Antrim and Down and was the remote cause of their later expansion into Argyll. The northern branch of the Uí Néill set up their power at Aileach, a hill which although only 800 feet in height still commands the valleys of the Foyle, Swilly and Deal and the northern loughs. The hill was topped by a prehistoric cashel (*caiseal*=stone fort) and it may have constituted a hill-fort of the heroic age. In the story, two of Niall Noígiallach's many sons, Conall and Eoghan, had conquered northwest Ulster. Each took land, Eoghan, the elder, creating *Tír Eoghain* (the land of Eoghan) which became the main kingdom in Ulster and was still held by O'Neills until the Flight of the Earls in 1607, and Conall acquiring all of Donegal (except Inishowen which Eoghan retained). Their descendants were known as the Cenél

Eoghain and the Cenél Conaill. The men of Tyrconnell and Tyrone continued to struggle for Ulster mastery right to the end of Gaelic Ulster.

The Ulaid's Tara, Emain Macha, for ever associated with the Ulster Cycle of heroic tales, home of Cú Chulainn and the Red Branch knights and site of the palace of the legendary Conchobar Mac Nesa, was destroyed by the Connachta around the year 450. This cashel had appeared as Isamnion in the famous map of Ireland, commissioned by Ptolemy of Alexandria in the second century AD. For nearly 1,500 years it lay desolate and mysterious as Navan Fort, but it has since been 'heritaged' and hints of its former glory, more mythical than factual, may be experienced. The destruction was part of the southern Uí Néill's campaign against the territory of the Airgialla (the 'hostage-givers') which included parts of south Tyrone, Monaghan and Cavan.

By the time of the coming of Christianity, Ulster, like the other provinces, had *tuatha* and over-kingdoms. Territories were fought over and jealously guarded. Since war and battles are remembered more vividly than years of peace, the history of the time seems troubled, but this is not necessarily a true picture. One thing is certain: the new faith was taken to with great rapidity and enthusiasm. True, wars and battles continued with warriors answering call of *fine* and *tuath.* (even the great St Colum Cille fought at Cúl Dreimhne in the battle between Connachta and the Cenél Conaill). Neither country nor province was to be united until after the British conquest of the seventeenth century. The Celts have left many legacies, mainly cultural, but the inheritance of their delight in local kingships and distrust of larger alliances was to make Ulster for all its natural defences comparatively easy game for the soldiers of a united England. True, the Britain and Alba of the sixth century AD showed the same characteristics, but who could have foreseen that the societal patterns imported from central Europe and codified by men with amazingly subtle yet rigid intellects should survive for a millennium. The Romans stopped short at Anglesey and their civilisation did not impinge upon the Celtic; the Roman Church, when it came, found itself as much influenced by its Celtic neophytes as influencing and the Normans did not do a thorough enough job in their partial conquest. The Celts left a mark on Ulster that was never quite erased, for all that Britain tried and tactically needed to do. In parts of the Ulster Gaeltacht their presence is still palpable.

– 3 –

SANCTI ET DOCTI
THE COMING OF THE FAITH

The story of the coming of Christianity to Ireland, like the lay history of the period, has elements of myth. These wonder tales which cling to the great saints of the period originated in later ages and, while it is easy to recognise occasions when piety was the inspiration, it is difficult to separate historical fact from parable. A symbol of this mixture of history and devotion is the alleged grave in the grounds of the Protestant cathedral in Downpatrick which is marked by a stone inscribed *Patric*. (It was commissioned in 1900 by Francis Joseph Biggar, the Belfast antiquary.) John de Burgo, the Norman lord who seized Downpatrick, is credited with the couplet

> In burgo Duno tumulo; tumulantur in uno
> Brigida, Patricius atque Columba pius.

This is usually rendered: 'In Down three saints one grave do fill, /Patrick, Brigid and Colum Cille.' All figure in tales of marvel, the stories of Colum Cille showing him quite choleric and St Brigid rendered as a cross between a pagan goddess and a Sister of Mercy.

The great name is Patrick, although there were Christian missionaries in Ireland before his time, and two documents

22

written by him in unsupple Latin have been scanned and analysed for autobiographical information about the apostle of Ireland. The *Confessio* mentions his birthplace as Bannavem Taberniae and says his Irish captivity was spent near the wood of Foclut. Much time and ink have been spent in identifying these places. Ulster people insist that it was on Slemish, a 1,500 feet hill rising out of the centre of the Antrim Plateau, that he served his time as a swineherd. It is generally accepted that he was born somewhere on the Severn shore near Bristol, that he was taken prisoner by the dreaded Irish raiders (tradition says by Niall Noígiallach himself), that during his six years of lonely exile he turned to God. He escaped in his twenty-second year and decided to become a priest. He trained in Gaul, probably with Germanus in Auxerre, which was then, like his native Britain, Roman and Christian, and returned to preach the gospel to the Irish. He landed, again according to tradition, in the year 432, a consecrated bishop, at Saul near Ráth Celtchair, later renamed Downpatrick in his honour, when he would have been about forty-seven years of age, and spent the rest of his life on his apostolic mission.

Most of the Patrician sites are to be found in the north and east of a line from Galway to Wexford. Apart from religious foundations, these include two places of austere pilgrimage: Croagh Patrick in Mayo, the 'Reek' that is climbed barefoot on the last Sunday in July, and St Patrick's Purgatory, the island in the lonely landlocked Lough Derg in southeast Donegal. The saint is said to have fasted for forty days and nights in each place, having visions of hell and purgatory and winning special favours for his beloved Irish children. The subjugation of the body that these traditions indicate was to be characteristic of the monastic Irish church in the next four centuries. The ecclesiastical organisation that Patrick himself devised was a copy of the church in Gaul, with dioceses run by bishops and secular parochial priests. He set up his headquarters near Emhain Macha, which has remained the primatial see of Armagh (*Ard Mhacha*) and managed accommodation with the Celtic kings. It is not likely that he actually clashed with the Ard Rí Lóegaire about the lighting of the paschal fire on the hill of Slane but it is true that this son of Niall Noígiallach offered no opposition to the new beliefs though he remained faithful to Druidism himself. In fact, although opposition to Christianity was stiff and long-lasting, there is no record of martyrdom. The baptised Irish, however, were no more popular with the Christians in Britain than they were as sea-raiders. Patrick's other extant work, *Epistola ad Milites Corotici*, chided the British prince Coroticus because some Irish converts had been killed by his men.

Patrick and his followers did not so much eradicate the system of beliefs they found as graft their faith on to it. He probably helped to recodify the Brehon Laws as Christian and his *Penitentials* were to remain a guide to moral satisfaction for centuries. They match the austerity of their deviser. The effect was to make the Irish church unique in Christendom and perhaps not in the way its main apostle intended. It was Patrick who introduced monasticism into Ireland and,

24

sanguine as he was, he still must have marvelled at the enthusiastic way the Celts took to the life. A century after his death, in the last decade of the fifth century, Ireland had become a monastic country with its most important churches having a hierarchy based upon abbacies rather than bishoprics. Even Armagh took on a monastic character with the bishop of equal or inferior rank to the presiding abbot.

The Irish monks tended to seek solitude even in their cloistral enclosures, living in bee-hive shaped huts and meeting for work, food and choir. The largest building would have been the church, and except in the barren west all these constructions would have been of wood. The 'campus' would have been decorated with examples of one of the artistic glories of the time: the free-standing high crosses which were Biblical visual aids. They became centres of learning both sacred and profane. The importation of church Latin gave the learned class, tending more and more to the religious life, a script in which to write down the Celtic epics. Till then their only system of lettering was the cumbersome Ogham which consisted of lines cut on the edge of a standing stone.

The result was a golden age when Ireland was a light in the dark ages. While Roman Britain fell to the ravages of Angles, Jutes and Saxons and north and east Scotland were pagan and Pictish, the Irish monks copied the scriptures in marvellous illuminated manuscripts of which the *Book of Kells* is only the most famous, taught the sons of the rich from all over Europe, helped to preserve the ancient classics (Adamnan of Donegal, the biographer of Colum Cille and one of his successors as abbot of Iona, knew his Virgil and Horace as well as any Oxford classical don) and generated a vernacular poetry which, with the written version of the heroic tales, constituted the earliest north European literature.

Teaching, copying, farming, fasting, giving praise to God, might have seemed sufficient occupation for even the most dedicated anchorite. Yet some monks sought the bleakest possible sites, the better to fulfil their vocations. Enda set up his monastery in Inishmore in Aran and there was a religious institution in Tory Island separated from the mainland by an even more inhospitable strait. Lonely as the life could be at river bends, deep in woods, on off-shore islands – in the case of Skellig Michael little more than a rock in the sea – the ascetic tenor of the Celtic monks demanded more. Some took to absolutely eremitical lives, copying the lives of the desert fathers. These anchorites are remembered in such placenames as Desertmartin in County Derry and Desertegney near Buncrana. For all the rigours they endured, which included corporal punishment (Columbanus recommended: 'Let the monks' food be poor and taken in the evening'), they were in Ireland and not that far from their homes and family groups. So to turn the screw of mortification some became, as they put it, 'exiles for Christ'. To these men so conscious of native place and family ties this was truly 'white martyrdom'.

One of the earliest and most famous of these '*perigrinatores pro Christo*' was <u>Colum</u> Cille. He was an aristocratic member of the Cenél Conaill, born near Gartan in central Donegal and founder of monasteries in Durrow, Swords and Iona. It is impossible to prove that he started the foundation in Derry but it would be unwise to deny it in the northern city that still bears his name as *Doire Colmcille*. There are many stories about the reason for his exile but the most likely and simplest explanation is that he too wished to suffer exile. His dabbling in politics which led to his participation in the battle of Cúl Dreimhne (in County Sligo near the foot of Ben Bulben) and his obvious connection with the Cenél Conaill would have made it difficult for him to have continued with his religious life had he stayed. He left Ireland in 563, by tradition from the narrows of the Foyle above Culmore with an apostolic twelve companions, and founded the famous monastery of Iona (a misprint for *Hy*). Except for an important attendance in 575 at the convention of Druim Cett (near modern Limavady and close to the monastic site of Drumachose) he spent the rest of his life in an island which, though nearly a hundred miles from Ireland, was quite central in the kingdom of Dál Riata. The convention was mainly to settle dynastic matters in the straddling kingdom but there is a charming tradition that under the heading of 'any other business' Colum spoke out on behalf of the poets whose bardic order had become corrupt and venal. The saint died in 597 and by then Iona had equal status with the leading mainland Irish sites.

The chief early foundations in Ulster were at Bangor, Movilla, Derry, Arboe, Kilmacrenan, Fahan and Devenish Island in Lough Erne. Movilla, founded c. 540 by Finnian who brought the Vulgate to Ireland, was Colum Cille's seminary, just as neighbouring Comgall's Bangor (founded c. 559) was Columbanus's. Columbanus, Gall, Fiacre, Aidan, Fursey, Fergal and Kilian all left to carry the faith to lands beyond their own beloved island, setting up houses in Luxeuil and Bobbio, St Gallen, Paris, Lindisfarne, Péronne, Salzburg and Würzburg. The church at home grew and prospered, church and state managing to live in tolerable amity. A majority of religious lived in settlements which were the nearest things to towns that the non-urban Celts ever experienced. They served as schools, hospitals, prisons, markets and religious and lay were not segregated. In fact the larger monastic communities were also universities and the fame of these learned *Scoti,* with their eccentric frontal tonsures and odd system of calculating the date of Easter, was for the time worldwide.

Less is known about religious institutions for women. The premier saint is Brigid, whose feastday, 1 February, is sig.nificantly close to the Celtic *Imbolc,* the beginning of spring. No Irish saint, not even Colum Cille, has such an accretion of wonders, and it is impossible to filter any facts from the mythology. She is said to have been born in south Ulster sometime in the sixth century, and to have had a monastery in Kildare for men and women, sharing the same church and ruled jointly by abbess and bishop-abbot. Other women whose names have come down to us are Ita of Kileedy and Moninne of Killeavy but they are descried, if at all, through a thick veil of mixed myth and hagiolatry. The independence of women which was such a feature of the heroic tales seems to have perished with Cú Chulainn and Fionn.

The age was truly golden. Learning was paramount and the artificers who used to make crowns and fillets for high-kings now also made chalices, croziers and shrines. Inevitably history books have tended to concentrate on the culture and learning of the period that caused the land of the Irish, once described by Columbanus as *ultimi habitores mundi* ('inhabitants of the world's edge') to become known as *insula sanctorum et doctorum.* Yet outside of the monastery palisades the fragmented patchwork quilt of *tuatha* continued. Even so small a region as Ulidia, as the territory of the Ulaidh was known, roughly the land east of the Bann, had three over-kingdoms, Dál Fiatach (mid-Down), Dál nAraide (the Lagan valley) and Uí Eachach Cobha (Lough Neagh and South Antrim) with many smaller units including Lecale, Ards and Larne. This pattern was repeated throughout the country. Attempts at establishing a highest king of all who would rule Ireland as continental kings ruled their lands came to nothing. Individual petty kings were too jealous of their own domains. There was no outside enemy against whom they needed to unite. So though Ireland had cultural, legal, religious and linguistic unity for nearly four centuries it was politically and militarily unsound. This freedom from aggression ended with raids in the year 795 on Rathlin Island in Dál Riata and Lambay in the territory of the Laigin. Ireland, having avoided conquest by Rome and escaped the Germanic incursions into Britain, was to suffer the attacks of the last barbarians, the Vikings, and for two centuries the fear of the white-haired Northmen and their long ships was to persist.

4

RAIDERS AND TRADERS
THE VIKINGS

The Northmen, *Lochlannaigh*, as they were eventually called, engaged in marauding activity during the ninth and tenth centuries, much as the Irish had in the third and fourth. Unlike the Celts, however, their main purpose was settlement and trade. The Scandinavians who attacked Ireland, especially the north, were from Norway. The Swedes turned their attentions to Asia and the Danes' sphere of activity was Germany, France and Britain. It is an irony of history that the Normans who defeated Harold at Hastings in 1066, mainly because his army was exhausted after overcoming a Norwegian army at Stamford Bridge a few weeks earlier, were of Scandinavian descent. It was these same Normans who were to have such a significant effect on Irish history both at their coming a hundred years later and much more direly in the sixteenth century, when the Tudors turned to Ireland for expansion and to mend the weakness in their defences against the forces of the southern European Counter-Reformation.

The Vikings were distinguished as *Fionnghaill* ('fair-haired foreigners'), the Norsemen, and *Dúghaill* ('dark-haired foreign-ers'), the Danes. The latter came to Ireland in the tenth century to strengthen and exploit the Norse 'Blackpool' settlement. They were mainly from northern Britain; Sitric of Dublin was also lord of York. Some member of the Irish-Danish chamber of commerce could very well have set up the medieval equivalent of signs saying 'Hurdleford twinned with Yorvick'. Certainly the other main Irish towns, Wexford (*Weissfjord*), Waterford (*Vethrafjorthr*, 'the ford of Father Odin'), Cork and Limerick owed their existence and their mercantile prosperity to the trading instinct of the Vikings which was even greater than their propensity for raiding.

They lived much the same kind of lives at home as did the Irish except that they were not yet Christian. Their gods were not unlike those of the early Celts and especially significant was their belief in Valhalla, the banqueting-hall where the souls of heroes killed in battle feasted for eternity. They were fierce warriors, well-qualified for Valhalla, and engaged in mutilations and blindings of their prisoners which the Irish at first found reprehensible but which they later adopted for their own local wars. They were farmers, carpenters, artificers and armourers and their spears, swords, shields and helmets were superior to those of their adversaries. The Scandinavian countries, especially Sweden, were rich in iron and copper, and the Norsemen were particularly good shipbuilders, navigators and marines. Erik the Red explored the Greenland coast and founded Norse settlements there, and his son Leif landed in 'Vinland', identified as America, about the year 1000. By the time they turned their attention to Ireland they were already well established in Iceland and nearer home, in Orkney and Shetland.

Their clinker-built ships with beautiful curved prows were oceanworthy and yet being of shallow draught could penetrate deeply into the well-rivered and centrally flat Ireland. When the waterways were too shallow or ran through rocky gorges their ships could be carried to the next navigable stretch, and when necessary they dragged them ashore to form the basis of a fortified stockade, much as the covered wagons of the American west were driven into a circle against the Indians. The placename Dunalong (*Dún na Long*, 'fort of the ships') six miles south of Derry on the Foyle suggests that a shipstead was created there. There are, however, not many Ulster placenames which show a Viking influence. Strangford ('strong fjord') and Carlingford ('hag's fjord') are obvious examples, as are the Skerries, the rocks off Ramore Head at Portrush. The English word Ulster came from *Uladztir*, a Viking word created from *Uladh* and *tír*.

The first raids were just that. One or two longships with sides armoured by rows of round shields and mainsails decorated with ravens or eagles would appear near a settlement, usually monastic, and murder, rape and looting would be followed by quick withdrawal. Because of Irish geography and Viking artifice, even the important midlands settlement of Clonmacnoise was not safe. Bangor, Devenish and Armagh were regularly pillaged during the first half of the ninth century. The Columban establishment of Iona, which had been a treasure house of spirituality and art for two hundred years, was raided at least three times between 795 and 806 when monks were slaughtered and the monastery treasures taken. In the end Cellach the abbot decided that

the site should be abandoned and retreated back home to
County Meath, leaving the great centre derelict. There in
a new monastic site near Kells the most famous of the
illuminated treasures of early Christian Ireland was preserved
and given its modern name. Many of the precious shrines
that held the relics of older saints (the Irish Church was just
as susceptible to the trade as that of the Mediterranean) were
taken back to Norway.

The Viking terror produced a famous doodle in the
margin of the ninth-century St Gall manuscript about the
benefits of a stormy night. The terrified monk who wrote
it was glad that the wind was whipping up the sea because
he knew that for that night at least the monastery would be
safe from the fierce foreigners. The monks were not in a
position to know about the Vikings' economic skills. To
them they represented murder and pillage, and what was
more heinous in the eyes of the religious, sacrilege. Sanctuary
meant nothing to the sons of Odin. Turgesius, one of the
early raiders who conquered Dublin and Leinster in 813,
made himself abbot of Armagh and was reported as doing
unmentionable things with his wife, Ota, on the high altar
of Clonmacnoise before she set herself up as a sybil there.

Eventually fleets instead of single ships began to appear.
Ireland was a prize well worth the risk with its short winters,
plentiful grass, horses and cattle, and its monastic treasure
houses. Since there was at the start no united stand against
the invaders, they quickly established their townships along
the east and south coasts. The only sizeable settlement in
Ulster was at Larne where Larne Lough must have seemed

like a home fjord. So too must Lough Swilly and though there are no Norse placenames in that area, it was later the territory of the MacLaughlins, a name which suggests a very close connection with the Norwegians.

In spite of general confusion and lack of a cohesive response to the foreigners the Ulster kingdoms had rallied sufficiently by the second half of the ninth century to offer resistance to the invaders. Áed Findliath, king of Aileach, defeated a force of Norse at Lough Foyle, and afterwards gave his daughter in marriage to Olaf of Dublin, who had became a Christian. From an economic point of view the northern Uí Néill were in a sense too successful in overcoming the Vikings and destroying their settlements on the Foyle. Derry would have been an ideal site for a northern town, perhaps another Dublin.

Elsewhere the age-old internal rivalry continued. It was reckoned that Feidlimid mac Crimthainn, the bishop-king of Cashel, the centre of Eóganachta power in the traditional southern 'half' of Ireland, Leth Moga, destroyed more churches than the marauders in his move against Tara and the Uí Néill of Leth Cuinn. The successful campaign of Áed Findliath's son, Niall Glúndub, against the Vikings was undertaken as much to establish his position as an all-Ireland leader as to drive out the foreigner. His army was the nearest to a national army ever mustered and certainly more representative of the two 'leths' than that which actually ended Scandinavian power. His army was utterly defeated and he and twelve other kings were slain in 919 at Kilmohavoc on the Liffey west of Dublin.

The Viking period lasted from late in the eighth century till the beginning of the eleventh when, in 1014, at the battle of Clontarf, Brian Boru defeated an alliance of Norse and Leinster men and there followed a period of peace and recovery. Apart from the loss of life, despoliation of property and pillage of church and lay treasure, the threat and the terror had had a stultifying effect upon both the saints and the scholars. Ireland was no longer the haven of sanctity and learning. The church had become in need of reform and there was a gradual secularisation of the monastic schools. The effect was of a lesser dark age, such as Rome and southern Europe had suffered earlier. Yet during the two hundred and odd years of recurring hostile interest the Vikings gradually became part of the *Politik* of the troubled island. They often made alliances and mutual-defence arrangements with Irish leaders, particularly those of Leinster, who were becoming important rivals to the Eóganachta and the Uí Néill. (In the middle of the ninth century, for example, Norsemen established in east Ulster made an alliance with the Ulaidh to defeat a force of Danes in a sea battle in Carlingford Lough.)

When Mathgamain and his younger brother Brian Boru, leaders of an obscure *tuath* in what is now east Clare, called Dál Cais, began their military careers it was the kingdom of Cashel that was their ultimate prize. Their reputations as saviours of Munster from the foreigners were obtained as a by-product of territorial expansion. Their total defeat of Ivar of Limerick at the battle of Sulchoid near Tipperary in 968 effectively ended the Norse power in the southwest. Ivar fled with the two Eóghanacht princes Donovan and Maelmuad, and Mathgamain ruled for a peaceful eight years as king in Cashel. Ivar and the Eóghanacht pretenders returned in 976 and killed the king by a ruse but they were quickly defeated by Brian. He thus became the most powerful leader in Ireland and had sufficient national support to proclaim himself *Imperator Scottorum* in Armagh when he visited the see in 1005 as part of a royal progress round the whole of the island, 'keeping the sea on his left hand'. Clontarf, the final battle, was fought against a united force of Vikings and Leinstermen by Munstermen with Norse support. The battle found its place in the Icelandic *Njal's Saga* because Vikings from all over the Scandinavian world including Iceland and Orkney, as well as from the coastal strip from Balbriggan to Arklow, which was known as the kingdom of Dublin, took part. Brian, an old man in his mid-seventies, was killed by Brodar, the King of Man, as all Irish schoolchildren used to know, just as the battle was won. The military power of the Scandinavians was at an end and Brian's body was conveyed with great solemnity to Armagh for burial.

Any power the foreigners may have had in Ulster had ceased seventy years earlier. Muirceartach, son of Niall Glúndub, ended the Scandinavian threat by turning sea-king himself. He defeated the Norsemen in Strangford Lough and raided Viking settlements along the whole west coast of Scotland until his death in battle, like his father and grandfather, in 943. Though the Vikings had met with stiffer opposition in Ulster than elsewhere they had still inflicted great harm. Bangor, Movilla and Derry never recovered. The primacy of Armagh led in time to the return of episcopal government. The appointment of the great reformer Malachy to the see in 1132 spelled the end of the Celtic liturgy and the coming of order monks to Ireland. He founded an Augustinian Priory in Downpatrick and built the first Irish Cistercian monastery at Mellifont in County Louth, in Airgialla territory. The days of the eccentric peripheral worship were over and Ireland, for the first time, began to feel the influence of a stronger kingdom on the other side of the Irish Sea.

5

THE LAND BEYOND THE PALE

In older popular histories when more respect was paid to individuals than today, the story of the coming of the Normans to Ireland had at least one operatic heroine, Dervorgilla, the wife of Tiernán O'Rourke, the king of Breifne. She has passed into a rogue's gallery of people who committed wrongs against Ireland that may never be forgiven. So potent a folk memory had persisted about her that Lady Gregory heard her story from her Kiltartan tenants and wrote a play in which she asked a pardon for her sins against an Ireland conquered by the Gall (= 'foreigner', as opposed to Gael). The play's last lines, given to a wandering 'songmaker', are:

> My curse upon all that brought in the Gall
> Upon Diarmuid's call, and on Dervorgilla!

Until her time the great Irish *femme fatale* had been Gormflaith who married in turn the Viking king, Olaf, the high king, Malachy, Brian Boru's greatest rival, and Brian himself and offered herself as wife to the Norse King Sigurd of Orkney as a prize for killing and defeating her most recent husband at the coming battle of Clontarf.

In 1152, Dervorgilla, then in her forty-fifth year, was abducted by Dermot MacMurrough, king of Leinster. It is generally held that Dervorgilla was more than willing and probably arranged the rape herself, but it started a relentless enmity between O'Rourke and MacMurrough that ended only with the latter's death. The episode was taken to be the first link in a causal chain that brought the English to Ireland and changed Irish history as radically as did the coming of Christianity. It was O'Rourke's humiliation in the eyes of the kings of Ireland and his expulsion of MacMurrough from his lands at Ferns with the help of Rory O'Connor, the high king, that caused the Leinsterman to seek help from the English king and started nearly a millennium of 'occupation'.

Another historical female character who played an important part in the events of this period was Nesta Ap Rhys, a princess from Wales. She had love affairs with among others Henry I, the Norman king of England and Stephen of Cardigan, and married Gerald of Windsor. In this way she became the founder of a sinister line of more or less disaffected Norman adventurers including the Fitzgeralds, the Barrys and the Carews. The Norman conquest of England had been swift and successful and now ninety years later Henry II was a kind of emperor of the west, lord of England, Scotland and Wales and most of north and west France. The Normans as conquerors were militarily efficient and, for the period, quite benevolent as colonists. Saxon and Viking settled down to help make the beginnings of a strong kingdom where the only foes were internal. The feudal barons had often as much might as the king and were as quick to sense central weakness as Irish kings were to register the instability of an *ard rí*. Henry, unlike his son John, knew how to keep them in their places by a judicious mixture of power and stratagem, and when Dermot of Leinster sought help against O'Rourke it seemed an excellent venture to engage the interest and greed of the Welsh marcher lords who were becoming restive.

The truth is that in medieval times with countries as close geographically as England and Ireland the stronger was inevitably going to have to come to terms with the weaker, either by conquest or by neutralisation, the latter best achieved by at least formal acceptance by the Irish of English overlordship. Henry's successors had as much trouble with Wales and Scotland as they had with Ireland. The king turned his eye on Ireland not long after his accession but was dissuaded from any precipitate action by his astute mother Matilda, known as the 'Empress Maud' because of her dynastic ambitions for herself and her sons. So the invasion of the country clearly visible across St George's Channel seemed a neat move, which would please Henry's ally Dermot and establish a bridgehead to which he would turn his attention later.

The leader of the Irish expedition was Richard de Clare, commonly known as 'Strongbow', and he had the promise both of the hand of Aoife, Dermot's daughter, and his kingdom of Leinster at his death. His foot-soldiers were mainly Welsh and Flemings who had settled in South Wales. The adventurers were essentially the twelfth-century version of their Viking forebears – except in savagery. They were magnificent soldiers equipped with formidable weaponry.

Their huge kite shields, chain mail and armoured helmets with characteristic nosepieces gave them a protection unimagined by the brave but disorganised Irish. Their Welsh and Fleming archers could work with devastating effect and the fact that their harness was equipped with stirrups meant that they were essentially cavalry, as they engaged foes who had to dismount before they could begin to fight with their swords. The superiority of British archers was to make them feared throughout Europe for centuries. The longbow was the ultimate weapon, winning Agincourt for Henry V 250 years later, and supreme until the coming of the cannon.

The Normans were formidable in battle and superb in defence of conquered territory. They covered Ireland with motte fortifications which formed the basis for stone castles, the remains of which still dot the countryside and provided the background for many sentimental Victorian prints and Boucicault backdrops. By the year 1300 they had control of most of the country, only the resolute Gaelic chieftains of Tír Eoghain and Tír Chonaill refusing to accept Gallic sovereignty. Well protected by their gallowglasses, the Scots-Viking mercenaries, they continued to allow themselves the luxury of such disdain.

Strongbow's venture was successful and, as Maclise's mammoth painting in Dublin's National Gallery portrays, he married Aoife and became Earl of Leinster. He held Waterford and successfully beat off attacks on Dublin, his capital, which was destined to be the centre of English power for 750 years. By 1171 Strongbow might have made himself an Irish king who could have found accommodation with the other leaders and been assimilated as painlessly as the mercantile Scandinavians. Certainly his closest colleagues would have been in favour of renouncing allegiance to Henry. Strongbow, for all his courage and military *nous,* was a vacillating politician and so, like Garret Mór Fitzgerald, the sixteenth-century Anglo-Irishman who might also have become a king of Ireland, he held off from making the decisive move.

Henry II was much better at statecraft, and as soon as he realised that the Irish adventure had been successful he headed for Waterford with an army of 4,000 men and the copy of the papal bull *Laudabiliter* to prove his moral right. This had been granted to him at his coronation in 1155 by Adrian IV, the only Englishman ever to sit on the chair of St Peter. It gave the land of Ireland to Henry in order to bring about 'necessary religious reforms'. (The legality of the grant was based upon an old decree of the Emperor Constantine, who stated that all islands were the property of the Church.) It was an odd card to play for a man who may have been responsible for the murder of Thomas à Becket the previous year, but it worked. Among those who hastened to accept his authority when his army reached Dublin was its archbishop, St Laurence O'Toole, who spoke for all the Irish bishops. (Strongbow was prevailed upon by the archbishop to build Christ Church Cathedral, where he was afterwards buried.)

Henry made his troublesome younger son, John, Lord of Ireland in 1177 and proceeded to parcel out Munster among his more demanding barons. For the next four hundred years Norman Ireland was an autonomy ruled by such magnates, who paid less or more homage to England. From time to time their lord, the reigning king, found it necessary to come in person to make sure that the fealty was more than lip service. John, who became king on the death of his French brother Richard I, considered it advisable to land at Waterford in 1210 with the greatest host that Ireland had ever seen. His descendant, Richard II, came with an equally impressive army in 1394 and secured Leinster, which had been occupied by the great Art Mac Murrough, the fourteenth-century scourge of the Gall. Before returning to a now troubled kingdom he received the homage of the Irish chiefs. It did not mean very much at the time since he had to return in 1399 to try unsuccessfully to enforce it, but it gave Henry VIII a legal argument for taking the Crown of Ireland in 1540. There would have been a closer regal attention paid to the country if the Plantagenet kings had not through the centuries had enough to occupy them at home. Most of the fourteenth century was marked by struggles with Scotland and trouble with Wales, and the Hundred Years War between England and France ended in 1453 only to produce the Wars of the Roses, which lasted from 1455 till the coming to the English throne of the first Tudor king, Henry VII.

As far as Ulster was concerned, the first fifty years of Norman involvement were the most significant. After that it was the land 'beyond the Pale' literally as well as figuratively. The term was first used to establish the 'land of peace' safe under English rule, as part of the agreement secured by Richard II in 1395, but by then Ulster had reverted to being an independent, Gaelic and intractable part of Ireland. She

43

took little part in the often stormy disputes that occurred in the other three provinces between the native Irish, the Anglo-Irish and the emissaries of the English throne and did not change her character until after the battle of Kinsale in 1601.

The first of the adventurers who left their mark on the northern province was John de Courcy, *Conquestor Ultoniae*, who began a highly effective campaign in 1177, the year of John's lordship, the more impressive in that he had only twenty-two knights and three hundred infantry. De Courcy occupied Lecale, the peninsula south of Strangford Lough which contained the Patrician site of Saul, and soon subdued east Ulster as far north as Fair Head. He set himself up as unauthorised *'Princeps Ulidiae'* (=Prince of Ulster) and confirmed his authority by the building of strong Norman keeps, notably at Carrickfergus on the north shore of Belfast Lough. The north coast he generously 'granted' to the Norman de Galloways who lived in Argyll, thus giving a quasi-official authority to the age-old commerce between northeast Ireland and southwest Scotland. He was officially religious, as were all his peers, and it was he who renamed Downpatrick and caused the so-called remains of the saints to be buried in the new cathedral. He established monasteries at Inch, Greyabbey and Coleraine and parcelled out the land of Antrim (as far east as Lough Neagh) and Down to his comrades, thus effectively founding the noble families of Hacketts, Russells, Whites, Savages and Logans. His thirty years of rule brought great economic advance and under him and his Norman successors, including his usurping rival Hugh de Lacy, there came into being the towns of Limavady, Newtownards, Portrush, Carrickfergus and the little hamlet of Le Ford which was later known as Belfast.

When John became king in 1199, de Courcy fell from favour. John established Hugh de Lacy, a son of his father's Dublin justiciar, as Earl of Ulster in 1205 after he had successfully driven out the former 'prince' who sued for pardon and became what he was before 1177, an ordinary Norman knight. Five years later de Lacy was himself expelled by the king after a successful campaign which included a siege of Carrickfergus Castle. De Lacy had sheltered the king's enemy Walter of Limerick and was shown by a triumphant John that he was his father's son. The earldom of Ulster (the old land of the Ulaidh east of the Bann) was to have a number of leaders including Richard de Burgo, the 'Red Earl', who built Northburgh Castle in 1305 on the shore of Lough Foyle just at the narrow mouth of the Foyle opposite Magilligan Point. It was captured by Edward Bruce in 1318 in his campaign after Bannockburn to set up a Scots-Irish alliance that would drive out any adherents of the English king, Edward II. He would rule as an independent king of Ireland with support from his brother Robert, who was undisputed holder of the Scottish throne. After some success his forces were finally defeated at the battle of Faughart and he was killed on 14 October 1318. The Red Earl recovered his lands and the Norman presence continued in Ulster and Inishowen until the death of Richard's grandson Walter, the 'Brown Earl', in a family feud in 1333.

The heirless interregnum that followed saw the gradual erosion of English power. Fifty years later the ancient Uí Néill clans were the dominant power in the north of Ireland.

with many parts of the centre of the old earldom occupied by the Clannaboy (later Clandeboye) O'Neills. The rest of the century saw the consolidation of O'Neill power and the continuing rivalry with the O'Donnells and for all of the fifteenth century the lords of Tír Eoghain were the northern equivalent of the Earls of Kildare, who dominated Irish politics outside of Ulster. The great Anglo-Irish families, Desmonds and Ormonds in the south, Fitzgeralds in the east, had become in the well known tag *ipsis Hibernis Hiberniores*, but this was only an English chronicler's view. The Gaelic chiefs beyond the dyke would not have accepted the description. The first of the 'Great' O'Neills made the same kind of accommodation with the representatives of Edward IV in 1449 as did Garret Mór Fitzgerald, and like him he made no response to the suggestion of Tadhg O'Brien, the Lord of Thomond, that he become high king and drive the English out. It was not in accord with the psychology of a Gaelic chief to consider the country as a whole as any of his concern. His interest extended just as far as his own territories. The gifts that he received from Edward IV were in token of his agreement not to attack the Land of Peace and to make sure that lesser chiefs of the south of the region, the O'Hanlons, the MacMahons and the O'Reillys, refrained as well. Unlike the Anglo-Irish he had little interest in the Yorkist-Lancastrian struggle, except, perhaps, to regard England's difficulty as his opportunity.

In 1485 Henry of Richmond defeated Richard III at Bosworth Field and brought the Wars of the Roses to a successful conclusion, though it was some years until people could be sure that the fighting was over. Henry VII might be thought to have looked askance at Fitzgerald because of his unswerving support of the House of York, even to the extent of sponsoring Lambert Simnel and Perkin Warbeck in their unsuccessful attempts to dethrone the Tudor king. The result was Poynings' Law, enacted in 1494, which was in effect an Act of Union and emasculated the Irish parliament until its repeal in 1782, when Grattan formed his independent government. The same packed parliament attainted Fitzgerald and he was lodged in the Tower of London. After the beheading of Perkin Warbeck he was released, Henry having already decided that 'since all Ireland cannot rule this man, this man must rule all Ireland'. He ruled Ireland as deputy till his death in a local feud with the O'Mores of Laois and his son Garret Óg succeeded him. By then there was a new king on the English throne.

Though Garret Mór might well have made himself King of Ireland and fulfilled the dream of many since Strongbow's day of driving out the Gall, he remained a King's man, advancing into Tyrone in 1498 with an army which included O'Donnells and Maguires, and imposing the King's Peace upon Niall, the current O'Neill chief. The Ulster he ruled in name was essentially divided into lordships, with O'Donnells chiefs of Donegal and Fermanagh and accepting the fealty of MacSweeneys in the west and south of Tír Conaill, of O'Dohertys in Inishowen and of Maguires in Fermanagh. Derry, Tyrone, Armagh and Monaghan were all in the Supremacy of O'Neill with O'Cahans, O'Hanlons, and

MacMahons as subsidiary clans. North Antrim was disputed by MacQuillans and the Scots MacDonnells, Mid-Antrim was ruled by the Clandeboye O'Neills and the Earldom of Ulster had shrunk to the land of Lecale, Ards and the country round Larne.

The north of Ireland had then been hardly affected by the Gall, and kept its Gaelic ways almost intact. Those Gaelic ways implied intense family loyalty but no great sense of national identity. Just as the fact that Ireland was never colonised by the Romans was not necessarily an unalloyed benefit, so too the lack of pervasive Norman and Anglo-Irish influence was probably to Ulster's disadvantage. Its concomitant disparateness made it an easy prey for the Tudor and Stuart armies. The acculturation which so characterised both the Pale and the lands of the Anglo-Irish had not taken place there. The schools and colleges and the medieval university in Dublin which advanced Gaelic learning were mainly the fruits of Anglo-Irish patronage. Only in church matters was the 'conquest' felt: the church was episcopal and the monasteries European. One Northern Gaelic prince who qualified for the description of Renaissance man was the sixteenth-century chieftain, Manus O'Donnell, whose work *Betha Colaim Chille* collated all the facts and fancies about the Donegal saint. The work was written at Lifford in 1532 and seems to demonstrate that if the Tudor conquest had not happened, a Gaelic-speaking Ireland, perhaps ruled by someone like Hugh O'Neill, might have evolved during the seventeenth-century and become a state as aware of the new learning and as fascinated by lands beyond the great ocean as other European kingdoms.

6

THE LAST PRINCE OF ULSTER

The virtual independence of sixteenth-century Ireland was finally shattered by Henry VIII. Unlike his father, who could have been reasonably regarded as a Welsh usurper, the king was a legitimate prince and popular with his subjects. Succeeding Tudor monarchs, whatever individual traits they may have shown, were all as hard-headed and thorough as the founder. They did not have Henry VII's flair for money gathering and retention but were quite as ruthless in maintaining and indeed furthering their positions.

Henry VIII engineered a characteristically English pocket 'reformation' and in his kingdom the Catholic Church ceased to be Roman. This was a significant change. The Gaelic Irish (and many of the Old English) remained faithful to the pope and so a further difference between conqueror and conquered was established and a further kind of 'disloyalty' could be adduced by English prosecutors. Ostensibly Henry's break with Rome was caused by a difference of opinion about the validity of his marriage to his brother's widow, who had produced only one surviving child. His determination to marry Anne Boleyn (a cousin of the Irish Butlers) and hope of producing a healthy male heir played their parts too but the main reason was personal ambition. He was determined to play an international role in Europe and the riches of the religious orders would supply the money for that perceived destiny.

His position as head of the Church of England (accepted in 1531) meant that he would become a target for the Counter-Reformation and the enemy of the guardians of Catholic Europe, particularly Spain. Ireland was to be his first external conquest, the beginnings of an overseas empire. A kind of *Pax Britannica* there would secure a possible weakness in his defences.

The 'Great' Earl's son, Garret Óg Fitzgerald, had incurred the enmity of Henry's chancellor, Cardinal Wolsey, as early as 1515 and he died in 1534 while incarcerated in the Tower of London for the third time. He had neither the strength nor the wisdom of his father, and his son, Thomas, the Tenth Earl, was unsuccessful in an uprising effectively forced upon him by this imprisonment and the appointment of Sir William Skeffington who superseded him as Lord Deputy. His followers were finally routed by Skeffington at his stronghold at Maynooth. As an indication of the new ruthlessness the survivors were given the famous 'pardon of Maynooth', that is they were all executed. 'Silken Thomas' (a sobriquet from the trappings of his bodyguard) himself was hanged, drawn and quartered with his five uncles in 1537, a promise of mercy given by Lord Grey, the new Lord Deputy, not being honoured by the king. The Irish had had their first taste of Tudor savagery. (Grey was himself executed by Henry four years later for his mismanagement of affairs in Ireland.)

These Leinster matters had little immediate impact on Ulster. The dissolution of Irish religious houses had been effected only in the towns of the Pale. The church in Ulster continued on its merry anomalous way. The old alliances and struggles between O'Neills, O'Donnells, O'Kanes, Maguires, MacMahons, MacDonnells, MacQuillans and the rest were maintained.

Henry's Irish ministers were not only efficient captains; they were highly competent administrators as well. They did not understand the structure of Gaelic society and the Irish views of such matters as land tenure and succession were frankly incomprehensible to them. (This was to have a significant effect on the comparative failure of the seventeenth-century Ulster plantation to carry out its work in full thoroughness.) In their efficient bureaucratic way they devised a system which they hoped would rub the slate clean and allow them to redraft it. Under the device of 'Surrender and Regrant' the Gaelic chiefs were confirmed in their holdings. Conn Bacach O'Neill, for example, became Earl of Tyrone in 1542, deciding that submission was advisable after the invasion of his territory by St Leger, the Lord Deputy. This submission included the recognition of Henry as 'King of Ireland', a new title which had been accepted by the Dublin parliament the previous June. This had for a time as little effect as the king's proclamation as head of the Irish Church in 1536. Yet the representatives of the last outpost of Gaelic Ireland had in fact accepted English suzerainty and by the end of Tudor rule, with the death of childless Elizabeth I in 1603, the conquest was effectively complete.

That conquest proved much more difficult than the English expected. Henry VIII was disinclined to waste any more money on subduing the north. He had his kingship and his supremacy of the church recognised by the civilised part of Ireland. As later monarchs were to discover, his frugal instinct about the cost of conquest in Ireland was sound. During the reigns of his successors, Edward VI and Mary Tudor, little change was effected in Ulster, though it was while Mary was queen that the first Irish land was 'planted': the territory of Offaly and Laois became King's County and Queen's County, a tribute to her husband, Philip II of Spain. The lessons learned from this venture were to have considerable significance for the future history of Ulster.

It was Elizabeth I who had the strength and determination to establish English rule. Elizabethan England was a buoyant country and by the social standards of the time an overcrowded one. There were many adventurers with enough brains, talent and ruthlessness prepared to do the queen's work. They had the morality of reformation on their side and the likelihood of huge profits, a combination which pleased everybody, especially the Puritans who were already growing in a strength which was to reach its zenith with the Civil War and the execution of Charles I, the son of the Virgin Queen's successor. Elizabeth was, however, pragmatic enough to prefer conciliation to a war of subjugation. She tolerated beyond the patience of her chief ministers the arrogant behaviour of Shane the Proud, Conn Bacach's son, who had himself declared The O'Neill in 1559, having driven his father into exile. He behaved as did many of his ancestors, engaging the Scots-Irish MacDonnells to the east and the

O'Donnells to the west. He also made forays into the Pale and regularly outmanoeuvred the Earl of Sussex, the queen's general.

Deciding again on conciliation, in 1562 Elizabeth invited Shane to London, where his exotic entourage became a nine-days' wonder. She was persuaded to approve his claims to the O'Neill territory and he was greeted as 'Captain of Tyrone'. Shane's rage against the MacDonnells and the O'Donnells continued. Like nearly all the Ulster chiefs of the period he could not see that the traditional internecine strife was greatly to the advantage of the English, who may have found the Ulster terrain horrendous but were masters of *Realpolitik* and as such inevitable winners. Shane was a cruel, vengeful man and his credit soon ran out. He had plundered most of the lands of the other Ulster chiefs, including those of the Maguires in Fermanagh, O'Reillys in Cavan and O'Hanlons in south Armagh. But his special rage was reserved for the half-Scots MacDonnell chief, Sorley Boy, whom he starved into submission at Dunluce Castle on the north coast.

He was finally defeated in 1567 at the battle of Farsetmore in east Donegal by Sir Hugh O'Donnell, his nephew, who led an army supplemented by MacSweeneys. The man the English had consistently failed to quell was overcome by more traditional enemies. Shane, with what seems a monumental lack of wisdom, threw himself on the mercy of the MacDonnells at Cushendun. Perhaps he hoped that Sorley Boy, who was still his prisoner, would act as a hostage. He was killed at a feast given by these hereditary foes and his head eventually spiked on the gate of Dublin Castle. His erstwhile prisoner was to survive for a score more years, to end his days as a loyal but still powerful chief of the lands between the Bann and the Bush rivers. In 1575 he had had to watch impotently from Tor Head while Norris, the Earl of Essex's most ruthless commander, massacred his wife and children whom he had sent for safety to Rathlin, and so was no friend to Elizabeth's captains. He had learnt, however, to play them at their own game.

The lessons of the nature of English policy with its exemplary savagery and perfidy were not lost on Shane's kinsman Hugh O'Neill, who was born in 1550, child of an illegitimate son of Conn Bacach. He lived in England from the age of nine, having been taken there by Sir Henry Sidney and brought up as an Elizabethan courtier in the new religion. He was confirmed as Baron Dungannon in 1568 and proclaimed Earl of Tyrone in 1585. For twenty years it seemed that he would behave as intended as an Elizabethan Irishman. He fought at the side of the English against Shane O'Neill and helped put down the Desmond rebellion in 1569. He was to be a controllable second 'great Earl' who would guarantee the safety of the Pale. In return he would have great power under ultimate English control.

It is not clear why he shrugged off this role: by maintaining even a token loyalty he might very well have secured the integrity of the Gaelic lands and won the right of Irish Catholics to practise their religion without penalty. He was a trained diplomat and a clever tactician, and seemed to be sufficiently statesmanlike to avoid the intemperateness that was held to characterise his peers, who with their armies of peasants and mercenaries could fight fiercely and well but could not reap the political harvest of their courage. Perhaps he understood that England was determined on eventual submission and expected to yoke Ireland and its nobility to her as indissolubly and as quiescently as Wales. His career was characterised on the whole by patience, courage and a sense of 'modern' statecraft. When in 1595 he went through the ritual (at Tullyhogue near Cookstown, where a prehistoric stone marked the place of inauguration) of becoming 'The O'Neill', the chief of Tír Eoghain, and therefore the premier Gaelic leader of Ulster and *de facto* of a risen Ireland, he had thrown down the gauntlet to Elizabeth, his late patron.

Her response, more in sorrow than in anger, was to have him proclaimed traitor and to send a succession of commanders to deal with him. On 13 June 1595 Sir John Norris was defeated at Clontibret, only the lack of ammunition of the winning side preventing the engagement turning into a rout. Three years later the combined armies of O'Neill, O'Donnell and Maguire inflicted a crushing defeat on the forces of Sir Henry Bagenal at the Yellow Ford, near Armagh City. O'Neill had married Bagenal's sister, Mabel, on the death of his second wife in 1591. Relations with his brother-in-law were never easy; there was trouble over an unpaid dowry, the husband's infidelity and a suspicion about O'Neill's true activities, as ever felt more deeply by the English in Ireland than by their monarch. Bagenal was killed at the battle and the Ulster alliance was for the time being successful. O'Neill's forces were rarely committed to pitched battles; they had no experience in line warfare and were chronically short of firepower. His main tactic was ambush and harrying the English forces on the march. He needed to have successes that would keep his often unruly alliance together and he knew that victory in Ulster would not be sufficient.

In 1599 Robert Devereux, the second Earl of Essex, son of the scourge of Sorley Boy, arrived with 20,000 troops to pacify Ireland. He met O'Neill and ignominiously concluded a truce after a stand-off at Aclint on the Louth-Monaghan border. He returned to England and started the spiral of disfavour and treason that ended in his death. The new Lord Deputy, Charles Blount, Earl of Mountjoy, was to prove O'Neill's nemesis. His policy of 'frightfulness' was intended to weaken and break the alliance. His strategy of burning crops and houses was symbolised by his destruction in 1602 of the O'Neill inauguration stone at Tullyhogue. In spite of famine, distress and the impatience of his allies, O'Neill still controlled an effective army. He needed to keep going until real help should arrive from Philip III of Spain. Knowing too of the queen's ailing health he wanted to have an army in the field when she should die, in the hope of better peace terms. When the Spanish forces under Juan del Águila did arrive it was at Kinsale, at the least effective and most distant port. O'Neill, against his better judgement, agreed to a formal battle and Mountjoy's forces won the decisive battle of the Nine Years' War.

O'Neill's chief colleague, Red Hugh O'Donnell, left for Spain immediately. His career was complementary to O'Neill but they were greatly contrasted. The son of Sir Hugh, Lord of Tír Chonaill, he was famous for heroic, almost glamorous, adventures: he escaped from Dublin Castle at Christmas 1591 after a three-year incarceration by Deputy Perrott. As chief of the O'Donnells a year later, he made effective inroads into Connacht and he joined with O'Neill to help secure the success at the Yellow Ford. His forced march over snowy Slieve Felim on his way to Kinsale added to his legend. It was probably he who persuaded O'Neill to agree to del Águila's demand for the pitched battle that proved so disastrous. The storybook characteristics stayed with him to the end: the following September he died by poison at Simancas while negotiating with Philip III. His old enemy George Carew whom he had eluded was, if not the instigator of the murder, certainly privy to it.

O'Neill made his formal surrender to Mountjoy at Mellifont on 30 March 1601 and learnt six days later with a mixture of sorrow and rage that Elizabeth had died on 24 March. Shakespeare's 'mortal moon' had at last 'her eclipse endured' and negotiations would have to be with the relatively unknown James I. The king had been reared as a Scots Presbyterian but he was the son of the flamboyantly Catholic Mary, Queen of Scots, whom Elizabeth had been forced to have executed. The new English (as opposed to the Old Catholics) in Ireland were in general Puritan and had many parliamentary allies at home. James's hand was forced by the discovery of the Gunpowder Plot (5 November, 1605) which helped to crystallise an anti-Catholic feeling among the English ruling class which they were slow to lose. Besides

Stuarts were not Tudors; they were at once vainer and less ruthless than the earlier dynasty and proverbially easier to persuade to break promises made to Irish Catholics. Already too the power of the English monarchy was notably on the wane. James I was the last ruler who was allowed to exercise it with Tudor confidence. Already a dichotomy between the monarch and his political retinue, and a new establishment of non-royalist landowner, was beginning to show.

In the aftermath of the Nine Years' War the English in Ireland expected at the very least public humiliation, if not actual execution, of O'Neill. They were furious to discover that he was effectively reinstated as Earl of Tyrone with many of his lands restored to him. Rory O'Donnell, Red Hugh's younger brother, was given similar treatment. The two leaders were placed under the personal protection of the king. Mountjoy, who was an able adversary of O'Neill in war, had become his friend at court. His death (3 May 1606) and a hardening of London attitudes was one of the causes of O'Neill's self-imposed exile. His successors, Chichester and Davies, made it clear that an Anglicised Ulster was their ultimate aim. They were two of the most able of James's men in Ireland and found it easy to persuade him that colonisation was the only means of pacifying Ulster. The logic and the manifest financial possibilities appealed to James, who had inherited severe debts from Elizabeth.

Characteristically neither side was faithful to the terms of the Mellifont treaty. Dublin continued the policy of imposing conquest and the new religion. In Ulster the Elizabethan policy of setting smaller chiefs against greater continued. O'Donnell was correctly suspected of being in 'treasonable' contact with Philip III and he grew steadily more fearful of discovery. O'Neill continued to show loyalty to the Crown, hoping to block Chichester's moves against him by using his credit with the king. Matters came to a head when Donal Ballagh O' Cahan appealed to London against O'Neill and O'Donnell realised that the best of his ancestral land had been assigned away, Inishowen to Sir Cahir O'Doherty and the fertile Lifford plain to Sir Niall Garbh O'Donnell. (The parading of these English titles added to the spleen of the erstwhile Gaelic princes.) Neither was prepared to go to London; there were many precedents of Irish chieftains who had entered the Tower of London by Traitors' Gate and never came out alive. What finally forced O'Neill's hand was the direct action of Cuchonnacht Maguire, the lord of diminishing lands around the Erne. Certain that the Crown servants in Ireland were determined to abase the Gaelic lords, he had planned a tactical withdrawal for more than a year before the Breton vessel which he had commissioned anchored at Rathmullan on the west shore of Lough Swilly at the end of August, 1607. O'Neill, O'Donnell, late Earls of Tyrone and Tyrconnell, with Maguire and nearly a hundred of the Ulster leaders, sailed past Fanad Head, establishing a pattern of exile which was to be repeated for a century. Gaelic Ireland was virtually dead and though the conquest was to prove lengthy and in fact temporary, the nature of Ireland and Irish life was changed forever. O'Neill settled in Rome, a papal tenant-at-will and pensionary of the Spanish king. He died on 20 July 1616 and was buried in the Franciscan church of San Pietro in Montorio.

If O'Neill had lived earlier he might have changed the course of Irish history. It is unlikely, however, that he would have been able for long to control and keep united his brother chieftains who in their pride and parochialism could never have been a match for a united England set on expansion. Within fifty years no Irish could own land except in Connacht and Clare and a century after O'Neill's death, as far as landowning and establishment were concerned, Ireland was essentially a Protestant country.

7

NEW FARMERS; NEW TOWNS
THE ULSTER PLANTATION

With O'Neill in exile and the remaining Ulster chiefs in disarray, there was nothing to prevent the colonisation of the province. James I, while retaining some benevolence and not seeing himself as a necessary advancer of the Reformation, was ready to leave the pacification of the contrary region to Chichester, his Lord Deputy and Sir John Davies, the architect of the plantation. Since the Irish could not be trusted they had to be removed from the land. By Irish the Crown officers meant the aristocracy. The ordinary people were regarded as insignificant; they would not be greatly affected by a change of landlord. Indeed they might have been totally acquiescent if they had shared the religion of the newcomers.

The 'flight' of the chieftains provided the Crown with large tracts of lands, deemed to be forfeit by reason of the treason of its holders. This included large areas of Tyrone, Fermanagh and Donegal. The Ulster territories had been 'shired' in 1580, as a first step towards the establishment of an English form of local administration, with the appointment of sheriffs. The counties chosen for clearance and plantation were Armagh, Cavan, Fermanagh, Donegal, Coleraine and Tyrone. Antrim and Down gave less reason for concern and in Monaghan the Irish power had been weakened by partition of MacMahon land among small chieflings of the name, making it an essentially 'native' plantation.

Antrim had traditionally been populated by Scots from Argyll and the Isles who hopped at will across the narrow sea, and Down at the time had a greater population of Scots than Irish. This was to have a significant effect later in the century when, as ever taking their religious and political coloration from Scotland, the loyal inhabitants became covenanters and for that reason important players in the notably complicated game played by Wentworth on behalf of Charles I. By the time of James I's accession these eastern counties were essentially if informally planted, with Lord Deputy Chichester holding land along Belfast Lough and the 'private' settlements of Hugh Montgomery and James Hamilton in Clandeboye and Ards officially approved.

The other counties were to be divided into lots varying from 3,000 to 1,000 acres, with the exception of Coleraine, which was to be the subject of a special venture that was to have a significant effect on affairs in the penultimate decade of the century. The undertakers were to be subscribers to the Oath of Supremacy, which guaranteed their religious orthodoxy, and were not to permit any Irish tenants on their lands. The church was to benefit too, as was the recently opened Trinity College in Dublin. In Donegal, for example, different tracts of land were assigned to English and Scottish undertakers, the new university, 'servitors' (worthy ex-servicemen) and loyal natives, and Inishowen became a prize for Chichester after the execution of the 'audacious traitor', Sir Cahir O'Doherty.

The stated purpose of all this was to impose segregation and 'civility'. The plan of erasing a Gaelic Ulster from the blackboard and drawing an English one did not succeed entirely. The towns were built, the forests cleared and the mires drained; the Black Pig's Dyke ceased to be a serious barrier to movement. But segregation proved inadvisable economically while impossible practically. The survey was mainly to blame. Irish land was reckoned not by area but by productivity. The Irish unit 'balliboe' (*baile bó* = 'pasturage') in spite of this was taken as sixty English acres, a gross underestimate. The larger unit, the 'ballybetagh' (according to the surveyors equal to the 1,000-acre which was to be the standard plantation unit) was in fact a tract with the *yield* of sixteen balliboes and, considering the generally unworked state of Ulster land, much larger than the 480 acres it was taken to be. The disaffected Irish were not only needed to work these huge areas but were willing and able to pay the rents. The plantation ballybetagh (*baile biataigh* = 'food-providing land'), too, tended to correspond to the Gaelic sept division and meant that old boundaries were seen to be retained but with foreign masters – the ultimate dispossession to be tenant of land that once you owned. Already the seeds were being sown for the bloody native response of 1641.

The planters were to have taken possession of their land by the autumn of 1610 and to have carried out the conditions of the grant within three years. By 1612 it was realised that the injunction forbidding Irish tenants was a dead letter. Many grants were to absentees whose agents had to employ natives, however unreliable. The newly impoverished Irish were on the whole quiet and made little overt complaint about their condition. Many of the undertakers were attracted by the chance of making quick profits and often resold their allotments without fulfilling any of the grant conditions. It is something of a generalisation but it could be said that the actual 'colonisation' was carried out by the Scots who took pride in the composite Presbyterian virtue of piety allied to industry. It was their work which changed the face and nature of the northern province. It was they who built the neat little towns, made what had been forest arable land and set up their chapels for sabbatarian worship.

The country dwellers built 'bawns' (*bábhún* = enclosure) around their farmsteads, making them into miniature forts because they dreaded the 'woodkerne' – their composite name for those of the dispossessed who had not acquiesced in the destruction of their country and the extirpation of the old aristocracy. Sporadic guerrilla activity was expected, and indeed occurred, from bands of soldiers still loyal to local chieftains. The threat, as often in such cases, was greater than the reality. Many native Irish landowners were allowed to keep a portion of their lands and the tenants were able to pay the often punitive rents imposed by the new lords.

The colonists varied in their treatment of the native Irish. In general the 'servitors', the veteran soldiers of the Irish wars, were reasonably tolerant and the nature of the plantation in their lands was not unlike that of other parts of Ireland where intermarriage was relatively common. The English opportunists were on the whole disappointed; there was a lot of hard work and if profits were eventually to come there was no immediate sign of them. The adventurers, like many others who were to colonise the New World, were often those who had not been successful at home: younger sons, failed businessmen and, in a considerable number of cases, near criminals. They were not likely to be patient and certainly not interested in proselytising, and it is certain that the respectable Scots would not have countenanced such an idea. Reconciliation was to play no part. William Allingham was to sum up their attitude two hundred and fifty years later in his long poem *Laurence Bloomfield in Ireland* (1864). The poem, by the man who could not bring himself to write a commissioned *History of Ireland* because of ' . . . hatred and revenge, blind selfishness everywhere . . . ' was written to explain the mid-century Ireland of landlordism and agrarian agitation, the legacy of these seventeenth-century plantations. He makes Larmour, the efficient Antrim doctor, dismiss the 'Kelts' (as Allingham called the descendants of the dispossessed) with:

> Walks the child a man?
> Or strays he still perverse and immature,
> Weak, slothful, rash, irresolute, unsure;
> Right bonds rejecting, hugging rusty chains,
>
> . . . .
>
> What Ireland might have been, if wisely
> school'd
> I know not: far too briefly Cromwell ruled . . .

The Ulster plantation was successful in that the north became 'different'. The neat, fortified farm became its visible characteristic where before there were forests and animal husbandry. The towns, built to formal plans, looked different from settlements in Munster, say. There were paved streets, strong houses, churches and schools. The Church of Ireland worshippers lived side by side with Presbyterians and, perhaps influenced by their nonconformist brethren, preferred a 'low' liturgy. The Thirty-Nine Articles began to seem to them quite 'Romish' and Calvin more than Cranmer became their preferred theologian. When, in the 1640s, sides had to be taken about support for king or parliament the 'conformists' did not take to Laud's high Anglicanism, and royalist support was not as great as might have been expected.

The most striking example of plantation was not the result of personal allotment but the creation of London merchants. The county of Coleraine contained territory along the east bank of Lough Foyle, including the little settlement of Derry which had an early fame as a monastic settlement in both Celtic and Norman times. Between 1566 and 1600 the English had made several attempts to establish a fortification there. The earliest one, that of Colonel Randolph, arrived by sea in September 1566 but the site was abandoned after a huge explosion. The effective establishment was the work of Sir Henry Docwra whose force landed on 15 September 1600 at Culmore, at the south narrow of the lough. He strengthened an already existing watch tower there and took over the town without resistance.

The settlement was in O'Donnell territory but the local chieftain was Sean Óg O'Doherty of Inishowen. His son Cahir had been prevented from accession because of his age; he was only fourteen when his father died. Docwra saw the chance of making a kind of minor O'Neill of the impetuous young man. He was received favourably by the queen, fought with such bravery against O'Neill at Augher that he was knighted, and was confirmed as Lord of Inishowen with castles at Burt and Buncrana. He was foreman of the jury that found O'Neill a traitor whose lands should be forfeit to the queen and might have had a loyal career as the king's Derryman if his patron had remained.

As it happened Docwra left Derry in 1606, disappointed at the progress of what was to be his own city. He sold his interests to George Paulett who had neither the finesse nor the integrity to continue Docwra's civic work. Paulett was vain and quarrelsome and soon made a mortal enemy of the hot-headed O'Doherty, publicly striking him during an argument over land-ownership. It was the end of O'Doherty's 'loyalty'. He mustered his forces, occupied the Culmore fort by a ruse and with arms obtained there marched on Derry. The town was fired, the garrison killed, including the irascible Paulett, and, in the tradition of the time, the women stripped and led away as prisoners. Many of the enemy had been acquaintances of O'Doherty, including the keeper of Culmore. Deputy Chichester, finding the Irish as ever 'more dangerous in peace than in war' condemned O'Doherty as a traitor. Risings in support by O'Hanlons,

O'Cahans and Sweeneys were eventually put down with fighting extending to the northwest as far as Aranmore and Tory. O'Doherty was killed in a skirmish at Doon Rock near Kilmacrenan in Donegal in July 1608 and his head was spiked outside Dublin Castle. Chichester graciously accepted the grant of his Inishowen lands. Strabane, Lifford and Derry had been reduced to near rubble and it looked as if the plans for a western city were to come to nothing.

Yet the location had always interested James I. He had been aware of its strategic position at the head of a navigable water system that covered a large area of northwest Ulster and one of the early enactments of his reign in England was to establish the city of 'Derrie', with Docwra as provost for life. O'Doherty had been one of its first aldermen. When Sir John Davies, the architect of the Ulster plantation, visited Derry in 1605, he noted that there were no recusants in the city and the loyal inhabitants earnestly wished for 'a new St Patrick'. The state of Derry after the O'Doherty rebellion was such that the most rational procedure was the building of a new town with enterprise capital.

One of the most persuasive aspects of the plantation scheme from the king's point of view was the hope of financial return. This did not materialise, at least not as rapidly as he had hoped. Derry was to provide him with readier cash. James made a suggestion (which had overtones of royal command) that the members of London companies, descendants of the medieval guilds, and immemorially jealous of their political and financial independence, should undertake the plantation of the county of Coleraine, which would become, with additions, a new county of Londonderry. Its chief town, which they should build, would have the same name. Articles of agreement were drawn up in 1610 after a survey by four representatives of the companies. The terms implied actual ownership of the lands, which was far from the king's original intention of some kind of sponsorship. The agreement was the result of an awkward compromise worked out between two strong parties. The city resented the element of command in the king's suggestion and secured in retaliation much more than James was originally prepared to concede.

The new county established in 1613 was granted a useful piece of land on the left bank of the Foyle and encroached a little east of the Bann to take in land that was originally part of Antrim. The barony of Loughinsholin, O'Cahan land in the southeast, was added to bring the county territory to Lough Neagh at Toome. The city was built to a classical plan with a rectangular layout of streets intersecting at a central market square. Walls were built right round the site, 1,700 yards in circumference, and so Derry (nobody used the formal name except for legal documents and and political argument) became the last medieval town in Europe and a place noted for the elegance of its design. Orphan apprentice boys from the companies were imported to increase the population and no native Irish were permitted to live within the walls. The management company which became known as the Irish Society originally intended the Londonderry enterprise as a profit-making enterprise, not unlike similar ventures in

Bermuda and Virginia. A cathedral founded in 1633 was the first Protestant cathedral to be built in the king's realm. Set in the the wall of the modern cathedral porch is the original foundation stone which commemorates the city's source. The inscription reads:

> If stones could speake
> The Londons prayse
> Should sounde who
> Built this church and
> Cittie from the grounde.

In 1616 Matthias Springham, who had surveyed the town for the Irish Society three years earlier, brought an ornamental sword for presentation to the city mayor and helped to found a free school which was sited near where the cathedral was to be built. This school, which was the ancestor of the present Foyle and Londonderry College, had as one of its pupils the dramatist George Farquhar, who attended the school in 1688.

By the time James I died in 1625 the plantation had 'taken' but nothing had quite worked out as intended. The lottery of portions to be assigned to the London companies turned out to be just that, with the Drapers getting much worse land than the Grocers. Towns such as Magherafelt, built by the Salters company, Draperstown and Moneymore, notable in having piped water by 1619 and built with 'the Sworde in one hande and the Axe in thother', Limavady and

Coleraine, rebuilt at the same time as Londonderry, had changed the appearance of the old O'Cahan country. The nine counties of Ulster were more or less at peace but the crucial exclusion of native Irish had not been achieved. The ordinary people had suffered a change of landlord but still survived, acquiescent if not content. They could not help regarding the newcomers as alien since they had a different religion and, more significant in the early days, a different system of tenancy. And they continued to live where they had always lived though under totally changed conditions, psychologically if not sociologically.

In fact the Gaelic aristocracy had not been entirely extirpated. Some members had made obeisance to the Crown and retained portions of their ancestral lands. Indeed there was no practical attempt at preventing their Catholic worship although it was official policy, and while many proclamations against Catholic clergy were made during the first four decades of the century they were rarely enforced. Some lords deputy were more active in prosecuting recusants than others. The Old Catholics tried to combine loyalty to their English monarch with loyalty to the Church and the pressures from Counter-Reformation forces in Europe made things difficult for them. The reign of the new king was to exacerbate their position considerably.

The twenty-four years of Charles I's reign were to gradually worsen the position of native Irish leaders and their hapless followers until the cataclysm of the Cromwellian campaigns and the total subjugation of the country. The planters, too, were to see their worst fears come true when the colonised rose in bloody riot. The events of 1641 were cleverly distorted and the number of deaths greatly exaggerated by Protestant propagandists ever since. The propaganda rather than the events left a mark on the settlers' psyche which has troubled them ever since. English and Scots gradually became indistinguishable in their attitude to the Irish. Their religions were nothing as far apart as those of the English and Scottish in their own countries, and they shared a mistrust of England. The Scots who settled in great numbers in Antrim and Down, with their homogeneity, their austerity and their increasingly evangelistic beliefs, soon began to dominate the planters' philosophy. They were always on guard against those who would injure their souls or their bodies, seeing conspiracy everywhere. Their sense of democracy and radicalism, existing even before the English Civil War, hardened during the decades that followed the Restoration but their egalitarianism did not extend to the native and Catholic Irish. They needed them still but mistrusted them all the more. A comparison with the plantation owners and their negroes in the southern states of America is not precise but it has some virtue. Certainly the troubled nature of modern Ulster was determined by the Jacobean plantation.

8

CHURCH, CHAPEL, MEETING-HOUSE
THE ESTABLISHMENT OF PROTESTANTISM

The Stuart kings were less ruthless than the Tudors but also less efficient, diplomatic and trustworthy. They were prepared to connive at the non-application of the anti-Irish, essentially anti-Catholic, statutes of their parliaments as long as there was no threat to peace and royal subsidies were paid. James I, who had been tutored by Scots Presbyterians, was easily the cleverest and best able to handle the growing power of the Puritans. His son, Charles I, who had little of his father's astuteness or good housekeeping, tried to manage without parliament, failed and was chronically short of cash. He was, like all the Stuarts, fond of favourites to the point of danger to them. His appointment of Thomas Wentworth, later Earl of Strafford, as lord deputy in 1633 was as much to have him collect much needed cash as to impose high Anglicanism on the Presbyterians of Ulster and the very low Church of Ireland.

Wentworth was not the man to create harmony in the troubled country but he did succeed in building up a Royalist army and an Ireland independent of the English parliament. He fined the undertakers of the city of Londonderry a hefty £70,000 for failing to evict the Irish from their lands in the city and county. He was not desperately concerned with this dereliction but he saw in their refusal to carry out the plantation conditions a convenient way of getting money for his royal master. It was said of him that he alienated every possible interest group in the country. His particular distaste was for the Scottish Covenanters whom he saw as the greatest threat to Charles. He recognised that the Presbyterians of Ulster were essentially of the same mind, indeed, in many cases kith and kin of the signatories of the Solemn League and Covenant. He knew too that only a moral inhibition would prevent their siding with the army that had menaced Charles at Berwick. He imposed on all Ulster Scots over sixteen the 'Black Oath', that they should not sign the convenant, but this was in fact null and void since he used his army to stiffen their resolve.

By the time of his recall, his eventual abandonment by Charles I and execution (in 1641) the passion that his presence had stirred was to act as a spark to set the flammable country alight. Catholics still retained 60 per cent of the ownership of the land of Ireland but they suffered severe penalties, social and religious. The Old English, as they were called, were promised amelioration of these conditions on payment of heavy subsidies to Charles but these 'graces' were never in fact granted. Wentworth had effectively wrested parliamentary control from them and given it to the New English, who though still loyal to the king (treason was a serious business) were decidedly puritan in cast and not all that different in attitude from Charles's parliamentary enemies at home and over the border.

On 22 October 1641 there were risings in Ulster and Leinster led by Sir Phelim O'Neill, the nephew of the great Earl of Tyrone, and Sir Rory O'More, who had extensive lands in the midlands. At first they were successful, in spite of their intentions, characteristically, being betrayed to Dublin Castle. About a thousand Protestants were slaughtered in Armagh, Cavan, Antrim and Fermanagh, and the insurrection spread to Louth, Monaghan, Roscommon and Sligo. By mid-November there were risings in Carlow, Kilkenny and Wexford, and the spring of 1642 saw the whole island up in arms and a success for the insurgents apparently close. Alarmed by an Ireland in flames England (and Scotland) at last took heed. On 15 April Major-General Monro landed at Carrickfergus with a force of 2,500 Scots to come to the aid of the Ulster planters. He showed the same mercy to the insurgents that they had shown the previous year. At the same time, James Butler, Earl of Ormond, the leader of government forces, began to turn the tables in Leinster. He defeated O'More at Athy on the same day as Monro landed. O'Neill was beaten by Hugh Montgomery on the Blackwater on 20 June. He was executed eleven years later, having survived the Eleven Years' War which followed.

O'More, who disappeared during the Cromwellian occupation, had played no very significant military part in the rising but had prevailed upon Owen Roe O'Neill to leave the service of the king of Spain and lead the Irish at home. Owen Roe landed near Doe Castle, the old stronghold of the northern MacSweeneys, and soon took command of the army of the Catholic Confederates. There followed a decade of an attritional war with continually shifting alliances. Though the armies which finally defeated the 1641 insurgents were Royalist, they soon found themselves at war with their fellow Scots and parliamentary English. The English Civil War broke out in August 1642 and England's difficulty could have been, but once again wasn't, Ireland's opportunity. The Irish Royalists made common cause with the Catholic Confederates but apart from the famous victory of O'Neill over Monro's Scots at Benburb, County Tyrone on 5 June 1646, where the Irish advantage was thrown away, the years of the Civil War were characterised by the forming and breaking of alliances, the gruel being made thick and slab by the presence of Rinuccini, the papal nuncio, whose Counter-Reformational zeal was not matched by sensitivity to local conditions.

The 'tyrant, traitor and murderer, Charles Stuart' was executed on 30 January 1649 and the enemy which the Irish had ignored, the English parliamentary army, led by the mercilessly efficient Huntingdonshire squire Oliver Cromwell, was ready to avenge 1641. Cromwell, who had attacked even the Presbyterians who wanted to make some accommodation with the king, was determined, and in the absence of any opposition able, to subdue Ireland once for all. He landed at Ringsend in Dublin on 15 August and captured Drogheda, Wexford, New Ross and Carrick-on-Suir before the end of November. O'Neill and Ormond made a belated treaty on 20 October but within a fortnight O'Neill's sudden death removed all opposition. (His successor, Heber MacMahon, Bishop of Clogher, was initially successful, capturing the garrison at Dungiven but falling to Coote at Scarrifhollis near Letterkenny on 21 June 1650. MacMahon was executed at Enniskillen on 17 September.) Cromwell or his generals, Ireton, Venables, Broghill and Coote, captured Belfast, Cork, Clonmel and Waterford. The war was over by 1652, the population having been reduced by plague, war and famine to less than half a million.

Cromwell's stay in Ireland lasted a mere 284 days but he remained the great Satan of Irish demonology for centuries, indeed until the late twentieth-century's combination of revisionism and historical ignorance. He was a superb soldier and utterly merciless in his slaughter of civilians of surrendered Irish towns. He had the Puritanical certainty of justification before Jehovah, and Catholics who resisted he pursued with the Lord's mighty sword. Besides, he had proof of their devilish cruelty in Sir John Temple's account of the Ulster atrocities, *The Irish Rebellion*, which was published in 1646. There certainly were grievously cruel acts perpetrated, especially in the early days of the insurrection. Derry, as later in the century, became a place of refuge for fleeing planters. The claim that eighty Protestants were driven into the Bann at Portadown to drown on 1 November 1641 is probably true, but equally well authenticated is the massacre of Catholics at Islandmagee the following January by Protestants, and the justification of the Monro army's policy of killing Catholic children: 'Nits make lice.' By twentieth-century standards the atrocities were negligible but the gross exaggeration of their extent has provided succeeding generations of politicians with a handy sectarian rallying-cry. Even the worst behaviour of Cromwell's soldiers was relatively minor compared with what we have become inured to and it should not be forgotten that their religious zeal was minuscule compared with their hope of gain. The magnates at home had plans for the confiscation and grant of all Irish Catholic lands, long before Cromwell's Biblical vengeance.

Most Irish soldiers and their officers were spared on condition that they take service abroad. About 30,000 took advantage of the amnesty. The ordinary people were on the whole left undisturbed to live much as before. The main feature which was not the same as before was that the Catholic Church was suppressed and the practice of religion became much more difficult. Yet it was in the devotion to the faith that the national identity was mainly preserved. Nothing else explains its survival through the blank eighteenth century and its recovery under O'Connell in the early years of the nineteenth.

The 'loyal' Catholic landowners had their lands confiscated but were given alternative, and usually smaller, holdings in Clare and Connacht; the others took to the woods and glens as 'rapparees' and 'tories' where most had colourful but brief careers as outlaws. 11,000,000 acres were apportioned to new settlers. In Ulster those Protestants who had taken the king's side in the war were fined but allowed to retain their granted territory, but even 'obedient' Catholics were relocated in Leitrim. Any remaining lands in the northern province not already granted were confiscated but in fact the arrangements made in the original Ulster plantation remained undisturbed. Any remaining moneys due from the Wentworth fines imposed on the Irish Society were waived and Cromwell himself restored its Londonderry property.

The Protectorate ended with the death of the Lord Protector and Cromwell's best general, George Monck, brought back the exiled Charles II. The condition of his restoration was amnesty to all but regicides and that in essence meant that the Cromwellian planters were confirmed in their acres. Charles II had had notable service from Irish Catholic aristocrats but he regarded his position as too insecure to undo any of the confiscations. (The career of his heir and brother, James II, indicates how precise his diagnosis of his situation was.) He had no special animus against Catholics (he admitted his own Catholicism on his death bed) and the anti-religious-practice enactments of Cromwell were not enforced during his reign. His appointment of Ormond (created an Irish duke in 1661) as lord-lieutenant was in general beneficial though it was Ormond's efforts that pushed through the Act of Explanation in 1665 which caused all claims about the ownership of Irish land to be stopped. He did prevent the anti-Catholic riots that characterised the England of Titus Oates's 'Popish Plot' but was unable to save the life of St Oliver Plunkett whose Irish and English enemies proved too strong. During his tenure religious orders began to return to Ireland and Masshouses replaced the rocks that had served for worship during Cromwell's regime.

In spite of severe restrictions imposed upon the export first of cattle and then all lifestock and animal products, Ireland began to experience some economic recovery. The Ulster towns began to prosper with Derry the largest (pop. 1,052 in 1659) and Belfast rising rapidly. The good land was heavily populated by planter stock but their native tenants, no longer seen as anything but a rhetorical menace, continued to live alongside. The rigid ethnic divisions weakened with intermarriage between the two traditions becoming fairly common, especially in western counties. A kind of exhausted peace had come and the condition of the poor was no worse than it had ever been. The Stuarts, however, had not yet finished with Ireland. The coming to the throne of the staunchly Catholic but politically inept James II was to bring yet more apocalyptic times to the most distressful country.

9

THE WAR OF THE THREE KINGS

James, Charles II's brother, became king in 1685 and from the very start of his reign acted as if his mission was to overturn the constitution and disestablish the Church of England. The alarm bells thus set ringing reached a climax in 1688 when a son, James Francis Edward, was born. By then plans were in place for James's daughter Mary and her Dutch husband William of Orange to take the English throne.

James's lord lieutenant, Richard Talbot (created Earl of Tyrconnel in 1685) who had survived the Cromwellian massacre at Drogheda, began an immediate amelioration of conditions for Irish Catholics. He was made commander of the army in 1686 and with reckless speed set about making its establishment almost entirely Catholic. He had already begun to restore Catholics to positions of authority in the towns. Protestant Derry ominously held out and it was not until August 1687 that the citizens accepted a corporation with a Catholic majority. All Ulster counties except Donegal were given Catholic sheriffs. The Protestants of the north stayed watchful as Catholic judges and privy councillors replaced 'loyal' incumbents but since there was no attempt made to repossess land they made no move.

The question of loyalty was a significant one. James was king, hedged even then by divinity, and it was hard at the start for the established Church to countenance a second possible regicide in forty years. Many of the purged officers sought service with the husband of the popish king's daughter, but the Ulster Scots, as ever taking their cue from their brethren across the straits, were inclined to give the Stuart the benefit of the doubt. James's record as administrator of Scotland during his brother's lifeime had been exemplary. Tyrconnel, though not quite as rash or tactless as his royal master, could not expect popularity with the powerful Protestant majority in England or the even more powerful minority in Ireland.

One response to his changes was the song 'Lillibuléro' written by the Williamite Thomas Wharton who afterwards as lord lieutenant claimed it whistled James out of three kingdoms. The first two verses without the refrain read:

> Ho, brother Teig, dost hear de decree
> Dat we shall have a new Debittie?
> Ho, by my soul it is a Talbot
> And he will cut all de English throat.

The refrain 'lillibuléro bullen a la' was a parody of the Gaelic warcry of the Catholics in 1641, and the supposed threat to the colonists in the extremely popular song was part of the anti-Jacobite propaganda. As ever, when England sneezed Ireland caught cold. By November 1688 William had landed at Brixham and was marching without resistance on London. James, who had decided it expedient to fly to the court of Louis XIV at the not-yet-completed Versailles, was held by the legalistic English to have abdicated. The struggle that began then was known in Irish as *Cogadh an Dá Rí,* but it was little more than one theatre of the war of the third king, Louis, in which the Grand Alliance of, among others, Spain, Britain, Holland, Austria, Bavaria and Pope Innocent XI did their utmost to stop his territorial expansion.

Talbot held Ireland for James and had control of a Catholic army to continue to do so, but in Ulster the Protestants were mobilising. An anonymous letter 'found' at Comber, Co Down warned that on 9 December 1688 the Irish would 'fall on to kill and murder man, wife and child . . . ' It was one of a number of bogus documents which, seeming to warn of another 1641, caused further tension. On 7 December the Catholic regiment of the Earl of Antrim, known as the 'redshanks', arrived from Limavady to replace the largely Protestant garrison at Derry. Their way was barred by thirteen apprentice boys who closed the Ferry Gate against the advance party. The other three gates were soon secured and the threat of cannon fire sent the Jacobite party back on the ferry to the east bank of the Foyle. The first significant resistance to the Stuart king had begun.

There followed the mythic Siege of Derry, which is premier in the achronological Protestant mantra, 'Derry, Aughrim, Enniskillen and the Boyne'. It has since then provided a bi-annual celebration for the Order of the Apprentice Boys and associates. The Closing of the Gates is remembered each 18 December (new calendar) with the burning in effigy of the 'traitor' Lundy, and the Relief of Derry each 12 August tries to outdo with drum and fife the anniversary of the Battle of the Boyne held province-wide a month earlier. The Maiden City became a Protestant icon and its siege, assuming a grandeur and a drama that it probably did not deserve, became the subject for much poetry (especially by the hymnologist Mrs Alexander and Charlotte Tonna), painting and of a polychromatic setpiece in Lord Macaulay's *History of England*.

It was not a classical siege with defenders holding an impenetrable citadel and constant battery by cannon and siege-engines. The gates were regularly opened and the investing Jacobite armies allowed many within to come out and refugees to enter. Lord Mountjoy, arriving with a regiment from Dublin, was not allowed into the city, but entered an agreement by which it would be garrisoned by a Protestant force. Lieutenant-Colonel Robert Lundy, a Protestant officer in Talbot's army, was appointed governor in March having been made to take an oath of allegiance to the new majesties, William and Mary, who had assumed the English throne after the 'bloodless revolution'. David Cairns, a Derry lawyer, had managed to persuade the new king to send arms, money and supplies and when he returned in the ship *Deliverance* he brought Lundy's commission with him.

James landed at Kinsale from France on 12 March 1689 and began discussions that were to lead to the setting-up of the Patriotic Parliament. This was to be a means of ruling Ireland that would give him a base for the reconquest of England. There was no suggestion of an independent Irish parliament; he made no attempt to repeal Poynings' Law. Crudely put, he intended to replace a Protestant oligarchy of doubtful loyalty with a Catholic one whose loyalty was unimpeachable. He had been reluctant to come to Ireland in the first place and was now even more reluctant to advance upon Derry. He was persuaded that his person was central to the struggle and that in the obscure northern town lay the one element of resistance to his rule.

An assault on the Catholic garrison at Carrickfergus had been effortlessly countered and one of James's abler captains, Richard Hamilton, had overwhelmed a Protestant force led by Arthur Rawdon at Dromore, County Down on 14 March and secured east Ulster. When Hamilton marched on Derry from the south he was met by a much superior force of defenders led by Lundy. They clashed at the fords on the Finn river about fifteen miles south of the city on 15 April and the Protestants were sent reeling back to Derry. Lundy was blamed for the rout and fell under deeper suspicion than before of not being an absolute anti-Jacobite.

The reluctant king presented himself at the south end of the city on the morning of 18 April, a day of characteristically heavy rain. His call to be admitted and have allegiance declared was met by gunfire and, according to the myth, shouts of 'No surrender'. He sat on his horse for most of the sodden day and when he withdrew the siege proper had begun. Lundy had defected from the city shortly before the royal débâcle and the fiery George Walker was appointed as joint governor. Defences were strengthened for the siege proper. The defenders had to face three and a half months of great privation and steady shelling. Though the city's walls were famously impregnable, the 'island' of Derry was surrounded by higher hills on three sides. There were several fierce skirmishes, at Pennyburn on 21 April, at an old windmill south of the city on 5 May and at Butcher Gate on 28 June.

The besiegers were outnumbered by the defenders and had much less firepower. They had no shelter from the continuous rain and being a chaotic mixture of English, French and Irish-speaking soldiers could not present a very disciplined fighting force. And all were surprised by the adamantine resolve of the defenders. When at the beginning of June, fresh Jacobite troops arrived under the command of the veteran French general, Marshal Rosen, the city was facing its greatest threat. He could have taken the place but with severe casualties to the citizens, and this would have been against the king's wishes. Hamilton, with the generosity and humanity that characterised both sides during the struggle, would not allow such a frightful option.

The Foyle, which flows past the southeast section of the city walls, widens out into a bay north of the city and then narrows again. At this place in the last week of May a boom of timbers and cables had been stretched across the river to prevent relief ships from getting upstream. The device had been designed by Pontis, the French chief of artillery, and he placed all his available cannon to defend it. It was a simple and effective means of blockade and the besieged citizens had the agony of being able to see a Williamite fleet led by Major-General Kirke anchored at Culmore but unable to relieve the city.

By the end of June conditions within the walls were atrocious, with hunger and disease the main killers. Horses, dogs, rats and mice were eaten and water was scarce. The city population was swollen with refugees and at the beginning of July the relentless Rosen rounded up all the Protestants from the surrounding districts and lined them up at the city gates, expecting the defenders to admit them for safety. He hoped thus to deplete further their scant rations, but again the humane Hamilton, following the specific instructions of the king that no Protestant not in arms should be harmed, sent them home again. There were many deaths in the beleaguered city and for months after the end of the siege cellars had to be cleared of corpses. Yet it was reckoned that as few as eighty people were killed in actual fighting. Among the attackers the loss of life was put at eight or nine thousand with thousands more wounded and a great number of desertions.

On Sunday 28 July the city governor, Walker, preached a kind of doomsday service in the cathedral urging his congregation to hold out and make any sacrifice to preserve the city. His congregation certainly included many Presbyterians, for sharp sectarian differences had been put aside for the duration of the fighting. (These were to break out again with great virulence later when Walker's bestselling *A True Account of the Siege of London-Derry* seemed to play down the Presbyterian contribution to the city's defence.) An hour after the service the sentinels reported that Kirke's fleet was on the move. The

Dartmouth engaged the Jacobite cannon, allowing the mariners in the *Swallow*'s longboat to hack at the boom while the *Mountjoy* and the *Phoenix* crashed through it. The ships made their way the remaining mile to the ship quay, running the gauntlet of the other Jacobite guns. Three days later, on 1 August, the siege was over after a sporadic cannonade. The armies of James II marched away and in Charlotte Tonna's words:

> . . . the Maiden on her throne, boys,
> Would be a Maiden still.

There had been no surrender and Protestant Ulster had her epic, complete with Homeric heroes including Michael Browning, the master of the *Mountjoy* who was killed by gunfire at the very moment of the breaking of the boom. As Lord Macaulay's fine flourish put it, 'He died the most enviable of all deaths, in sight of the city which was his birth place, which was his home, and which had just been saved by his bravery and self-devotion from the most frightful form of destruction.'

On the same day as the siege of Derry was ended a Protestant force from Enniskillen defeated Lord Mount-cashel's Jacobites at Newtownbutler. Their war cry heard for the first time in Ireland was specific: 'No Popery!' A confused order caused the Jacobite cavalry to retreat and their foot-soldiers were driven to the Lough Erne shore to die by drowning or slaughter. Two and a half thousand of Mountcashel's men were killed and he himself was captured, though he later managed to escape. The land of Ulster west of the Bann was secured for William and when Schomberg, his commander-in-chief, landed at Ballyholme in Bangor Bay on 13 August it was without opposition.

It was almost a year later that James II fought his last battle, at Oldtown on the Boyne on 1 July 1690. His mixed force of Irish and French amounted to 25,000 but William had 36,000 men and much greater firepower. The battle was won by the superior force and among the dead were Schomberg and the Reverend George Walker, the hero of Derry. It was a mighty victory and is celebrated as such by Orangemen every July. James, to his eternal shame among the long-memoried Irish, left the battle early, but the war was far from over. The *Te Deum* sung in the Stephansdom in Vienna was not, contrary to popular belief, authorised by the new pope, Alexander XVIII, though he had the same good reasons for being antagonistic to Louis XIV as his predecessor.

It was Aughrim's great disaster fought on 12 July 1691 that was the decisive battle of the War of the *Two* Kings. The chief Jacobite general was St Ruth, who had been the scourge of the Huguenots after Louis's revocation of the Edict of Nantes in 1685. He held a commanding position and was probably about to rout Ginkel's Williamite army when his head was carried off by a cannonball. Patrick Sarsfield, the grandson of Rory O'More (of 1641), who had emerged as the charismatic leader of the Irish Jacobites, fell back to Limerick, the scene of his brilliant successes of the previous year. He surrendered on the terms of the later repudiated Treaty of Limerick on 3 October 1691. 14,000 Irish soldiers including the mythopoetic Sarsfield left Ireland for service abroad, the first of the 'wild geese' who for the coming century 'spread a grey wing on every tide.'

The terms agreed by William, who was not a vindictive man, were not ungenerous but the Protestants in England and the even more vociferous Protestants in Ireland would not ratify them. The native Irish were left leaderless and debased, to become Swift's Yahoos, not exterminated because their labour was needed, but in every other possible way degraded. The seventeenth, the 'worst', century which began with Kinsale and ended with Limerick, had seen hopes raised only to be dashed and finally witnessed the extirpation of first the Gaelic, then the Catholic, aristocracy. The history of the Irish people from then on was to have a terribly different character.

10

WAITING ON DUBLIN
THE PROTESTANT NATION

With the ending of the Williamite war Ireland was at peace and indeed, apart from agrarian outrages, was to remain so for a hundred years. The eighteenth century saw a remarkable increase in population, five million in 1800 compared with two and a half million in 1690, and the estimated 500,000 when Cromwell ended the Eleven Years' War. Ireland was now a variegated country as to population. Apart from native Gaelic Irish there were Catholic Old English and a significant and empowered Protestant minority consisting of the Elizabethan, Stuart, Cromwellian and Williamite planters. This minority had two distinct groups, the Episcopalian ascendancy and the mainly Presbyterian nonconformists.

The Catholic majority consisted of surviving landowners and a large population of labouring, mainly rural, poor. Their drudging lives showed no great difference from that of earlier centuries. Even the English colonists were distracted briefly from their acquisition by the miserable condition of these little more than serfs. The Normans and the Gaelic chieftains who were influenced by the newcomers' feudal system replicated the baronial manor pattern which left the churls at subsistence level when not in arms for their lords. In Ulster, where the Normans' rule was brief, peripheral and evanescent, the life of this lowest class had this difference:

unlike the case of earlier generations they were tenants of alien landlords instead of having a position, however menial, in a patriarchal system that was subtly unfeudal. North and south they were seen as a possible menace and the ascendancy policy was to keep them in subjection. And as successful empire-builders, the authorities knew that the neatest way was to deprive them of leaders. In this they were successful for many years – indeed until a change in contemporary ideology and the collapse of the economic system which kept them in acquiescence caused them, however sluggishly and reluctantly, to generate their own effective representatives.

William III soon discovered the limitations of his power as a constitutional monarch, when he found it impossible to persuade the Protestants in Dublin and London to accept the terms of the 1691 Limerick treaty which gave Catholics such rights of worship as they had enjoyed in the reign of the last Protestant king, Charles II. He would have been content with such confiscations as the treaty gave him and reckoned that with the departure of the Irish Jacobites 'to wear the fleur-de-lis' the military threat was gone. In this he was proved correct and he might well have predicted that the leaching of the bravest and best would continue for the next century, with the gaggle of wild-goosery estimated as 250,000. Yet since the colonists had come in waves, the latest draught barely *in situ*, and since the seventeenth century had seen such alarums and changes of fortune, the Protestant ascendancy had a less than total feeling of security in their holdings and were not in the mood to risk anything. William was still at war with France and, though the Counter-Reformation drive in Europe had been dispersed in a welter of national Gallicanism, the threat of invasion from Catholic Europe was regarded as an ever-present nightmare. Whether the authorities in London and Dublin actually believed that the new Irishry on the continent would intensify anti-British feeling, it gave them the excuse they needed for the series of penal laws that would render the Catholic majority politically inert.

Estimates of Catholic landowning show a decrease from 22 per cent in 1688 to 14 per cent in 1691. By the end of the eighteenth century this had dropped to a low of 5 per cent and these holdings were mainly in Connacht where some of the survivors of the Cromwellian dislocation had against all the odds held their granted acres. (Edward Martyn of Tulira, who with Yeats and Lady Gregory started the Irish National Theatre, was one such, as were the Martins of Ross until two generations before the birth of Violet, the partner of Edith Somerville. Some Catholics accepted the new faith for the sake of their tenants but a remarkable number held out and impoverished themselves and their descendants.) With rare exceptions the motive for the 'popery code' was not religious fanaticism but greed. The anti-clerical elements in the laws were not in general vigorously prosecuted and certainly less so than in Britain. It was the economic debilitation that was grievous and effective in its purpose.

In Ulster there were virtually no Catholic landlords left though the condition of the aboriginal population was, especially east of the Bann, probably better than elsewhere. Catholics may have been degraded, deculturised and leaderless but they had learned survival. They offered higher rents for holdings than Protestants, often a cause of dissension and riot. The majority of Protestants, being Presbyterian, could not subscribe to the various 'test' acts that the Anglican Church, at its 'highest' during the reign of James II's second daughter, Anne (1707–14), was able to command. Their loyalty was assumed but their disabilities, though significantly less than those of Catholics, were real. The North Channel was still an inland sea to them and they were Scots in politics, religion and husbandry, and during the century they were in touch with and strongly influenced by the American colonies.

Emigration to them was not the wrench it was to the rooted Irish and the part played in the creation of the United States by Ulster Presbyterians has been well documented. The elements of personal effort, egalitarianism and devoutness that characterised their faith (in scandalous contrast to the hierarchical, and often worldly and boorish, Ascendancy Church) did well in the New World. The need for religious and social freedom, the absence of which they regarded correctly as persecution, was one spur, though economic factors played their part too. Their holdings were small and the population was growing very rapidly. Recurring harvest failure, notably in the mid-1740s, and resulting famine, became a kind of dress-rehearsal for the major shifts of the 1840s. The improved quays in Derry made it the premier port for this eighteenth-century emigration, with reports of twenty-five ships leaving in 1729, 3,000 emigrants using Derry in 1759 and similar numbers in the 1770s. These were mainly Presbyterian, although there were Anglicans and Catholics among them.

The Penal Laws (the last of which, dealing with Catholic disenfranchisement, was not passed until 1728 in the reign of George II) prevented Catholics from bearing arms, educating their children or owning a horse worth more than five pounds. (Any Protestant could insist upon obtaining that amount for a horse in Catholic hands – the most elegiac case being that of Art O'Leary whose death in Macroom on 4 May 1773 in a fight after such a transaction produced from his wife, Eibhlín, the aunt of Daniel O'Connell, the famous poem 'Caoineadh Airt Uí Laoghaire'. Abraham Morris, the High Sheriff, who had insisted on the letter of the moribund law, had O'Leary shot by his military bodyguard because of threats to his life but the absolute harshness of the beginning of the century had gone and Eibhlín contrived to have the members of the picket transported while Morris himself was killed by O'Leary's brother.) The professions, including the army, navy, all public offices and the lucrative legal professions were closed to Catholics, though they were allowed to, and many did, become doctors. Most effective in weakening their economic power was their inability to buy land and the dissolution of primogeniture, unless the heir accepted the Test Acts. (The oath required was so blasphemously offensive that no devout Catholic could take it.) Catholic land was gavelled among sons (or failing sons, daughters) until it was worthless and even then a near relative who had conformed could bring a 'discovery' suit and claim the land as his. The government's preoccupation with landowning as the economic index left Catholics (and Presbyterians) free to survive and eventually prosper as merchants. In this way a Catholic middle class was born and lived to bring its oblique power to bear on politics as the century advanced. Some of this mercantile prosperity was based on a 'smuggler' economy in remoter parts of the west from Donegal to Kerry. The basis of the Derrynane O'Connell wealth was illegal trade in liquor from France and Spain.

The anti-religious enactments drove all bishops, order clergy and non-registered priests out of the country, but active religious persecution lasted less than a decade. By the death of the extreme episcopalian, Anne, Mass was freely celebrated and except in occasional dioceses where there was an especially splenetic bishop or places where papists 'bulged' and needed a reminder of their subject position, there was a kind of tolerance. The 'persecution' of Catholics was considerably less virulent than in England. Apart from such pre-Reformation strongholds as Lancashire and the western Highlands of Scotland, Mass was celebrated there only in the chapels of European embassies. The low-level nomenclature of calling Catholic places of worship 'chapels' dates from these years and there are relics of the practice to be found in older streetnames.

In the north there was less tolerance among Presbyterians of 'popish natives' than from Church of Ireland communities, always provided that the tithes were paid. Memories of Catholic perfidy were kept alive, as ever for political reasons, and though egalitarian ideas, native and imported from America, were to find fertile soil among Presbyterians and lead to the founding of the Society of United Irishmen of Belfast in October 1791, the specifically anti-Catholic Orange Order was founded with active if clandestine government encouragement in Loughgall four years later. An 'Orange toast' recorded by Jonah Barrington, the chronicler of the more rackety side of the 'Protestant century', began: 'The glorious, pious and immortal memory of the great and good King William: – not forgetting Oliver Cromwell, who assisted in redeeming us from popery, slavery, arbitrary power, and wooden shoes. May we never want a Williamite to kick the **** of a Jacobite! and a **** for the *Bishop of Cork*! And that he won't drink this, whether he be priest, bishop, deacon, bellows-blower, grave-digger, or any other of the fraternity of *the clergy* . . . '

Eighteenth-century travellers from Arthur Young to John Wesley could not help but be struck by the different appearance that the neat farms and well laid-out towns of Ulster presented. The houses, too, had windows and chimneys, and the scene was not unlike that they were accustomed to in England: ancient villages with Norman square-towered churches, alms-houses, inns and greens upon which cricket had been played from the fourteenth century. In Ulster, however, the greens were much more likely to be bleachgreens, a part of the linen industry which was responsible for great economic advance in the northern province. Even as Charles I's manipulator, Wentworth, was imposing the Black Oath on the Ulster Scots he was encouraging the linen trade. Ulster kept its reputation as the 'safe' area, in contrast to its sixteenth-century reputation as the lawless Gaelic tract beyond the Dyke. Once covered with woods, it had become by 1700 the most deforested part of Ireland. Yet the wetlands thus exposed were found to be suitable for the harvesting of turf (or peat, as the Scots who first realised its potential as both fuel and rough building material, preferred to call it). And it was in Ulster that the new root vegetable from the New World was first cultivated.

The fuel fed the kilns and the potato fed the linen workers. The domestic industry became mechanised with the advent upon invitation by William III of the Huguenot, Samuel-Louis Crommelin, to Lisburn in 1698. He brought with him skilled workers, refugees from Louis XIV's persecutions, and became 'Overseer of the Royal Linen Manufacture of Ireland'. His *Essay* on his trade published in 1705 gave details of new skills and methods in use in France. His name survives in the village of Newtown-Crommelin in mid-Antrim.

Ulster had its premier industry and it generated others. Coal was discovered in sufficient quantities at Brackaville near Dungannon to make it briefly a good investment. The name of the place became Coalisland and as late as 1924 coal was mined there (but at too great expense). The mining caused the first industrial canal in what was then blithely called the British Isles to be built from Lough Neagh to Newry, opening for navigation in 1742. Ulster was not to prove a rich source of raw material apart from flax but it had developed an industrial character and entrepreneurial cast of mind which fitted in with the beginnings of the agrarian and industrial 'revolutions' which so characterised Britain from the mid-century onwards. It was able to share in Britain's lead over the rest of the world in manufacturing and this helped to make Belfast a nineteenth-century industrial city out of very unlikely raw material.

Not all of Ulster was equally prosperous. Donegal, apart from some individual investment in the fishing industry on the west coast and in Inishowen, remained undeveloped and the majority of its people were poor. They were subject to intermittent scarcity of food and some near-famines during the century. Those from the bleaker parts of Inishowen and Fanad tended to move towards prosperous Derry in search of work, and by 1800 there was a sizeable cabin population outside the western walls in what became known as the Bogside. The city had benefitted from the appointment to the diocese of the 'Earl Bishop' in 1768. Frederick Hervey was a liberal, a son of the 'enlightenment' and not such an absentee from his living as George Berkeley, the philosopher who was Dean of Derry from 1724 to 1732 but visited the city once. Hervey made Derry, already the plum living in Ireland, much more profitable, increasing the value of its rental by £13,000 a year not by rackrenting, a charge of which other clerics were guilty, but by good housekeeping. He built roads, churches and the first bridge across the Foyle. His contribution of £500 to the building of the first post-Reformation Catholic church was much the largest and he prevailed upon the Protestant corporation to give £50.

It was, on the whole, a century not characterised by liberal thought. The position of farmers was better than in other parts of the country because all tenants, whether Church of Ireland, Presbyterian or Catholic, had identical conditions of tenure, dating from the Plantation. Eviction could not be carried out at the whim of the landlord and there was some security as long as rents were paid. The two communities lived together in watchful distrust, the one finding the other's folk practices alien but interesting. There was some intermarriage and the coexistence was on the whole peaceful. The Catholics still spoke Irish and continued to do so until the early decades of the next century. Thomas Davis, the founder of Young Ireland, estimated (in an essay in the *Nation* called 'Our National Language') that west of a line from Derry to Waterford (a north–south boundary) Gaelic was still the first language though it was rapidly disappearing in the east. This preserved a minimal Gaelic culture since, apart from music and dancing at which (unlike their unco pious neighbours) they excelled, the Irish had a carefully preserved oral tradition of heroic tales of a glorious past that helped to prevent the degradation that their subject position might have caused. They also had their faith which, in Sunday sermons and low-key theological discussion, provided in many cases a form of adult education.

The long peace at home was disturbed by the revolt of the American colonies in 1775 though Ulster had had its own whiff of grapeshot when in 1760, during the Seven Years War with France, Carrickfergus had been held for a week by the French general, Thurot. In 1778 the notable

American privateer, John Paul Jones, had appeared off the Copeland Islands in his ship *Ranger* and seized the British ship *Drake*. The northern Protestants naturally sympathised with the revolutionaries – kith and kin again – but when the old enemy France joined the Americans and seemed about to invade England through the Irish backdoor they too rallied to join the Volunteers, an independent Ascendancy force, distinguished more by sumptuous uniforms than by fighting ability, that had seemed to burst into spontaneous life in the year of Jones's Irish adventure. Protestant Ireland was awake again and self-consciously aware of a possible independent existence.

11

VIVE LA RÉPUBLIQUE!

Even before the emergency caused by the French involvement in the American revolutionary war, there was a growing sense of Irishness among some Ascendancy Protestants. This group, led by Henry Flood and James Caulfield, Earl of Charlemont, constituted the opposition in the venal Dublin parliament and was spurred mainly by the trade restrictions that Irish manufacture had to suffer. These men also had a strong sense of affront that the (to them) ignoble London parliament and its puppets in Dublin should have such a say in Irish affairs. They still represented Protestants and had no special interest in Catholic emancipation. Flood in particular was formally against it. The performance of politicians in the second half of the eighteenth century in England could not be said to give good example and George III, the first English-born Hanoverian, was as autocratic as any Stuart. Dublin was in the process of becoming the Georgian showplace that so impressed visitors by the century's end and Belfast too was showing signs of an intellectual and aesthetic self-consciousness generated by its economic success.

The position of Catholics showed an agonisingly slow improvement. They were allowed to hold non-commissioned rank in the army and many indeed joined, as such songs of the period as 'Shule Agra' and 'Johnny, I Hardly Knew Ye!' indicate. They were allowed to hold longer leases in bogland

and no hindrance was made to their building their own churches, provided they were in side streets in cities and a sabbath journey outside the largely Protestant towns. When Flood fumbled in mid-career, Henry Grattan became leader of the opposition party and though much more conciliatory to Dublin Castle and the British parliament, understood that his dream of an independent Ireland required in justice and in policy an amelioration of its majority downtrodden population. In other parts of Europe subject groups were as degraded and powerless as the Irish Catholics but none of these constituted a large majority of the total population.

The founding of the Volunteers increased interest country-wide in the idea of separation. It also frightened the government in London. In 1778, the year of the English Catholic Relief Act, the Volunteers paraded in Dublin with their cannon which had a placard on its barrel with the words, 'Free trade or this!' A year later the trade restrictions were all but abolished but by then nothing less than legislative independence would satisfy the Volunteers. The American war ended at Yorktown in 1781 and the following February a delegate convention of the Volunteers met at Dungannon to demand the repeal of Poynings' Law and the Declaratory Act, more commonly known as the 'Sixth of George I'. A providential change of government at Westminster led to the Volunteers getting their assembly and from 1782 to 1800 there sat in the splendid buildings in College Green what has become known to history as 'Grattan's parliament'. It was characterised by self-conscious oratory, limited power and the passing of a series of legislative measures that removed some of the more grievous disabilities of Catholics. In 1782 they had education rights restored; ten years later they were again allowed to practise law. 1793 saw the founding of the first Catholic seminary, St Patrick's College, Carlow, and in 1794 Catholics were permitted to attend Trinity College. (One of the earliest of the new alumni was Thomas Moore, the son of a prosperous Aungier Street grocer, who became a close friend of the revolutionary Robert Emmet, and who in later years and in his own way sang to sweeten Ireland's wrong as effectively as some of the more strident balladeers.)

The Paris Bastille fell on 14 July 1789 and 'bliss was it that dawn to be alive . . . ' There were supporting demonstrations in Dublin and Belfast and the cries of *liberté* and *égalité* found an echo among the young Irish intellectuals. One of them, a young Dublin lawyer called Wolfe Tone, published a pamphlet in 1791 called *An Argument on Behalf of the Catholics of Ireland*. He, like many others, had grown impatient with Grattan's loyal gradualism and responded readily to an invitation from the liberal coterie in Belfast. The pocket northern city was prosperous and in a ferment about the ideas from France and the need for reform. Tom Paine's *Rights of Man* ran through seven Irish editions in 1791. Nearly all the radicals were Presbyterian and, debarred from Trinity, found their education in Scotland, notably in the 'enlightened' Glasgow university. Tone was welcomed by William Drennan, his brother-in-law Samuel McTier, his wife Mary and Samuel Neilson, the group that later founded the *Northern Star* as their broadsheet. The Belfast Society of United Irishmen came into being on 14 October 1791. Its members were mainly young, professional and mercantile in the city, and warm farmers in Antrim and Down. The only working-class leader was Jemmy Hope, the Antrim weaver and the only aristocrat, Hamilton Rowan. (He like Daniel O'Connell was in Paris during the Terror and both were cured forever of recommending armed revolution.)

One of the automatic aims of the Belfast club was full political rights for Catholics, though few of the majority religion were United Irishmen. Most were too poor and too concerned with survival to have the time or the inclination for political activity. Pitt, who had become prime minister in 1783, dreaded an alliance between them and Presbyterians and allowed Grattan to continue his coffee-spoon amelioration of their condition. In 1795 a bill was proposed that would remove from them the last political disability and give them the right to sit in parliament. Pitt was for the time an honest politician – he probably earned the proposed epitaph: 'he died poor' – but his precise, almost mathematical mind never quite grasped the complexities of Irish politics. (He was only the first of many well-meaning men who found themselves in the same position.) For most of his seventeen-year career as Britain's chief minister his main concern was France and the need to defeat Napoleon. He refused permission to grant emancipation, almost certainly because he was holding that card in reserve as a palliative for the union which he saw as inevitable.

The United Irishmen, north and south, were grievously disappointed but a majority of Protestants in Ulster, mostly

Episcopalian, were delighted. The idea of improving the condition of Catholics was abhorrent enough but the existence of an unchallenged Protestant radical society was unthinkable. The period was marked by agrarian turmoil and crude secret societies. The Catholics, not permitted to bear arms, had gathered themselves into a loose organisation called the 'Defenders'. Their Protestant rivals, known as the 'Peep o'Day Boys', were much better armed and from 1786 carried on an often vicious sectarian campaign which spread to rural Armagh, Monaghan and Cavan. The Defenders were not simply the rabble of rustic Catholic cattle 'houghers' that even the city radicals considered them. As many members were drawn from towns as from the country and they were often skilled workers. Their determination to make a stand against their Protestant tormentors was evidence that the long sleep of acquiescence was over. They too had caught a whiff of Jacobinism. On 21 September 1795 two rival mobs met at a crossroads near Loughgall called locally the 'Diamond'. The Armagh chapter of the Peep o'Day Boys, with local knowledge and superior firepower, won the encounter and thirty Catholics were killed. The victorious Protestants marched into Loughgall and in the house of one James Sloan set up the Orange Order. It received strong support from the Church and, with trappings and secrecy not unlike those of freemasonry, has persisted to the present day.

There followed a kind of religious war, more in the grand old spirit of the seventeenth century than that of enlightenment. Many Catholics were driven into Leitrim and Mayo, while those with more spirit and fewer responsibilities joined the United Irishmen, which had received the accolade of being banned. By 1797 the membership in Ulster was reckoned as 117,000 but as many Orangemen rushed to join the yeomanry from 1796 on. A loyal and anti-Catholic (and anti-Presbyterian) army was just what Westminster wanted and there seems no doubt that both the institutions were created with the active connivance of Dublin Castle and Westminster. As ever the British government's intelligence was excellent: their spies and informers had successfully infiltrated the radical associations. Tone had found it expedient to leave for America in 1795 after he was implicated with a French agent but the next year found him in France and successful in obtaining an effective expedition that sailed for Bantry Bay in December. Bad weather dispersed the forty-three ship fleet and the 15,000 men who might have taken Ireland for the Directory returned home.

In March 1797 General Gerard Lake began to carry out his commission to disarm Ulster with efficient enthusiasm. Indiscriminate floggings, burnings and killings soon removed any real threat of a successful uprising by the now unconstitutional United Irishmen. A typical case was that of William Orr, an Antrim farmer, who was charged with 'administering unlawful oaths' and in spite of a spirited defence by John Philpot Curran and the jury's recommendation to mercy was executed in the town. No attempt was made to disarm the Orangemen, and Lake left behind him a subdued province. Still the news of risings in the summer of 1798 in Dublin, Kildare, Carlow and Wexford spurred the remaining leaders to action. Henry Joy McCracken, a fiery young Belfastman, whose impetuosity and dedication to the cause of liberty had already caused the family linen business to fail and who had joined Tone, Thomas Russell and Neilson in the Cave Hill Oath, tried to capture Antrim but was defeated by Colonel Durham. He hid out for a while in Colin Glen and in Cave Hill until his sister Mary Ann could arrange for a ship to take him to America. He was captured by the Carrickfergus militia and eventually hanged on 17 July in the Cornmarket in Belfast, close to the tavern in Crown Entry where the Society of United Irishmen was formed.

The other Ulster rising began on 8 June at Ballynahinch in Co Down about fifteen miles from Belfast. The insurgents were led by Henry Monro, a Lisburn linen-draper. He held Montalto for three days but he was finally defeated by General Nugent, who had previously carried out his threat to set fire to and totally destroy the towns of Killinchy and Saintfield. Monro was hanged in Lisburn opposite his own front door and in sight of his wife and children.

The policy of frightfulness continued. The news from Carlow and Wexford told of atrocity on both sides and caused many in the north to abandon all trust in armed uprising. In all 30,000 people died in the months of July and August in that year of revolution. There was a final flicker in the west when General Jean Humbert landed at Killala and had some initial success over Lake's forces at the famous 'races of Castlebar', but he was soon surrounded at Ballinamuck. In November Wolfe Tone was taken prisoner off a captured French ship, the *Hoche*, in Lough Swilly and taken ashore at Buncrana. He was sent to Dublin, condemned to death and died seven days after a bungled suicide attempt. He slit his windpipe instead of his throat; as he whispered with characteristic aplomb to his surgeon, 'I find I am but a bad anatomist.'

Pitt was now determined that the only solution to the continuing Irish question was political union. He could offer the Catholics what he had withheld in 1795: full emancipation; and the horrors of 'Ninety-Eight', as it was forever known, persuaded many that constitutional struggle was kinder and perhaps just as effective as insurgence. Grattan was never more eloquent, but Pitt, publicly genial, used every effort to persuade by inexorable logic and plentiful bribes the members of the College Green parliament to accept unionism. The Orange Order opposed it, dreading 'popish democracy' and preferring the guaranteed Protestant institution. The bill passed the lower house by a majority of sixty-five and in the Irish Lords by twenty-five votes. The Act of Union became law on 1 January 1801 and unionism was born. Grattan had said in his final speech, 'Yet I do not give up my country; I see her in a swoon, but she is not dead. Though in her tomb she lies helpless and motionless, still there is on her lips a spirit of life, and on her cheeks a glow of beauty.' New actors were already in the wings who would revive the sleeping beauty.

– 12 –

'BOUND FOR AMERIKAY'

The history of nineteenth-century Ireland is dominated by the land of Ireland: its eventual change of ownership, its inability to support an ever-growing population and its place in the hearts of the many who felt they had to leave it. In Ulster the story was as ever somewhat different from that of the rest of Ireland. It was not as grievously affected by the great hunger of the 1840s, its system of land tenure, the Ulster Custom, was different from that prevailing in the other three provinces, and though there was much emigration the reasons for leaving and the eventual settling places of the emigrants were not quite the same as in the country as a whole. The other characteristic of Ulster life, some might wearily say the defining trait, was recurring sectarian conflict.

In Ulster the painfully slow improvement of the condition of Catholics was not regarded, as in the rest of the country, as probably a good thing if not very important, but as a matter of serious alarm and an occasion of regularly recurring sectarian riots. At the beginning of the century Catholics, though politically null, were in a majority in many of the thirty-two counties but in Ulster the population broke down into equal numbers of Catholics and Protestants. The Protestants, atavistically suspicious, found it hard to take the gradual enfranchisement and growing prosperity of the tolerated, when not despised, underclass, and as such were comparatively easy to manipulate. Their religious and political leaders could always appeal to fears of a kind of economic 1641 and they were equally susceptible to Tory manoeuvre. When Lord Randolph Churchill wrote in 1886, '. . . the Orange card would be the one to play' he was simply (and unwisely) putting into words a regular Westminster practice.

The union should have been abhorrent to the egalitarian Presbyterians who had supported if not actually fought for the United Irishmen. Yet within twenty years of the passing of the act all but the most radical had accepted it. The beginning of the century saw an increase in zeal in all denominations, Catholics included. John Wesley had been a regular visitor to Ulster – he came to Derry ten times between 1765 and 1789 – and had been impressed by the size of his congregations. The horrors of the armed uprising after a peaceful century were an element in bringing people back to fervour, and such a charismatic figure as Henry Cooke found a more than willing following in his move to reconcile Presbyterianism with the Dublin and Westminster establishments. His only rival in eloquence was Henry Montgomery, his exact contemporary, who spoke for a more liberal tradition and was an advocate of Catholic emancipation. He and his followers, known from the late eighteenth century as New Light, were expelled from the assembly by Cooke's followers in 1830. (They formed their own synod, known since as the Nonsubscribing Presbyterian Church.) The almost automatic association of Protestantism with unionism was due largely to Cooke's efforts, since he effected a working partnership between Anglicans and

Presbyterians and in a spate of sermons and pamphlets convinced a large majority of Protestants that not only security but economic prosperity was guaranteed by unionism. In a sense, however, no single figure, however possessed of charism, could persuade people against their deepest instinct: all preaching is to the converted.

The Church of Ireland was the more easily persuaded to accept the wedding of church and meeting-house, since it too was experiencing its own evangelical renewal and tended to a much more Calvinistic outlook than the Anglican Church in England or even Wesley would have approved. It was still the established church and until Gladstone's Act of Disestablishment in 1869 it was due tithes from all, whether members of the communion or not. (This church tax was in fact mitigated by a tithe act in 1838 but it was still resented.) In Ulster, although people of both of the main Protestant traditions were to be found throughout the nine counties, in general Presbyterianism predominated in Antrim, Down and Derry, while Tyrone, Donegal, Armagh and the southern counties tended to be Church of Ireland.

The Catholic hierarchy in so far as it had a voice to be heard did not actively oppose the union. Pitt had promised emancipation as one of the advantages but many, including George III, found that clause unacceptable and it was dropped. Most of the other penal disabilities had already been removed: there was no longer any attempt to prevent worship and the Royal College of St Patrick at Maynooth (1795) was added to that in Carlow as a permitted higher education establishment for the education of Catholic clergy.

One of the first Catholics to become a lawyer after professional disability was removed was Daniel O'Connell, the nephew and heir of a childless Catholic Kerry landowner sufficiently prosperous to have him educated in France and London. He was called to the bar in 1798 and soon established himself as one of the cleverest lawyers in the country. By 1814 he had found a political role as leader of the Irish Catholics. He had church and bourgeois support but his great following came from the degraded underclass, the peasants and urban poor whose numbers had increased alarmingly since the middle of the eighteenth century. He was, to use the title of Sean O'Faolain's biography, 'King of the Beggars', and with their monthly penny rent was able to finance the Catholic Association and win in 1829 the emancipation denied to Catholics by Pitt's opponents.

Emancipation removed the last civil and religious disabilities from all nonconformists including the Presbyterians but no gratitude was shown to the Liberator in Ulster. From 1829 until his death all of O'Connell's energies were directed towards the repeal of the union. He came to Belfast in January 1841 but did not take up his mirror image's challenge to open debate. Cooke and O'Connell were classical adversaries but they never met and O'Connell was to find, as many other well-meaning visitors, that Ulster, especially unionist east Ulster, was indeed a different place. His visit was low-key and greeted by well-orchestrated street protests and a pointed sending of more than two thousand dragoons and policemen to prevent 'counter arrays' getting out of hand. The tenor of the province was Protestant and the army and the constabulary were not even-handed in their keeping of the peace.

The Orange Order had had several vicissitudes since its triumphal founding in Loughgall in 1795. Then the spur to sectarian conflict was the perception by erstwhile independent Protestant linen weavers in County Armagh that the new mill system had degraded them to the level of mere employees while the status of many Catholics, especially in the towns, was clearly rising. When the Catholic Association was forbidden in 1825 under the Unlawful Societies (Ireland) Act, the Order was banned too but quickly reappeared as the Loyal and Benevolent Orange Institution of Ireland. An event similar to the Battle of the Diamond occurred at Garvagh in July 1813 when Catholic Ribbonmen (the successors to the Defenders) were routed by an inevitably better-armed band of Orangemen. The local magistrate said he did not dare call out the yeomanry because he knew they would simply have joined in the attack. In 1828 when Lawless, O'Connell's Ulster lieutenant, arrived in Ballybay to preach repeal, 8,000 Orangemen arrived to defend the union. The Catholics of Armagh pleaded with Lawless not to come to their town, his next stop, and when he agreed the armed Orangemen ran wild, discharging their muskets and generally behaving in a frightening and offensive way. In 1849 a number of Ribbonmen were killed in an affray at Dolly's Brae near Castlewellan in County Down. It began after a 'traditional' Boyne anniversary march but the only casualty on the Protestant side was a policeman who had been wounded by a bayonet in the arm by one of his comrades as they charged the Ribbonmen on the hill. The day's proceedings were followed by the traditional attacks on Catholic homes. The result was a new Party Processions Act but Orangeism remained a resilient and eager body ready to defend 'freedom, religion and laws' whenever their political masters required a confrontation or riot to bolster agitation or counter what was perceived as Catholic advancement.

By mid-century Catholics from Donegal flocked to Derry, and Belfast too had to accommodate a great influx from rural east Ulster. Both Catholic and Protestant brought with them a grand old tradition of sectarian enmity. The two largest Ulster towns were regularly to be the scene of civil strife rooted in suspicion and ignorance of the true nature of the other faction. Apologists for the Orange Order have defended it as a folksy society, its activities mainly social, but its many parades and shows of strength have often led to civil strife. Recurrent rioting and firing of houses provided accurate barometric readings of political pressure and sectarian fears. The order and similar organisations, such as the Apprentice Boys of Derry (founded 1814) and the Black Preceptory, continued to make the marching season a period of inevitably increased civil tensions. Most Protestant politicians found membership of the Orange Order an advantage and it remained an objective correlative of militant Protestantism.

Yet Catholics and Protestants did live for at least three-quarters of the year in reasonable amity. Not all Protestants were members of the Protean order and intermarriage especially in the west and south of the province was not uncommon. Ulster Catholics too tended to be politically rather quiescent, showing much less fervour over repeal or land agitation than was common in Munster and Connacht. This passivity can be understood when one reads in the 1861 census that 96% of Ireland's Presbyterians and 51 per cent of its Anglicans lived in Ulster. These are post-Famine figures but the changes in population brought about by that cataclysm affected mainly Catholics, and for the first time in the history of emigration from Ireland Catholics were in a majority of those who sought better lives abroad.

Emigration had been a fact of Ulster life since the eighteenth century when large numbers of mainly 'Ulster-Scots' left for colonial America and played a vital part in the revolution. The prosperity of Derry was partly based on its port, which was then the premier Irish point of departure. During the 1820s and 1830s ships from New York, Charleston, Savannah and New Orleans (and in summer from Canada) would discharge their flax seed and cotton and return with human cargoes. It is no wonder that Derry 'Kay' played its part in many emigrant ballads, though the rhyme with the local pronunciation of 'Amerikay' was probably irresistible. It is reckoned that up to 1.5 million Irish left home in the years 1815–45 and that figure had doubled in the years to 1870. Not all emigrants crossed the Atlantic. Indeed the Donegal practice of travelling to Scotland to help with harvests enabled some people to escape the worst privations of 1845. Fares to Britain were very cheap; Ulster emigrants could make their way to Liverpool and Glasgow for a few pence. Sometimes this initial break led to wider travel but many settled and set up in British cities the same pattern of sectarian location as at home in Derry and Belfast. Liverpool began to have its 'Twelfth' marches and the foundations for the ritual Glasgow Rangers–Celtic football-match confrontation were laid. However though most large British cities had areas informally designated as Irish there was little of that kind of internal strife. Most had a real if limited anti-Irish prejudice to contend with.

The apocalyptic Famine of the 1840s affected Monaghan, Cavan, Fermanagh and Donegal more than the other Ulster counties, though all were touched by it. Conditions in Cavan were as grim as anywhere in Munster and Connacht. Derry city found itself flooded with refugees from Donegal from 1846 on. As Edward Maginn, the Catholic bishop, noted in the summer of 1847, the Catholic population of his diocese was 230,000, of whom 50,000 were literally starving. The toll of death from hunger was terrible but it was slight compared with that caused by typhus, relapsing fever and the bacillary dysentery caused by famine diet.

The story of these years will continue to be told since it is so terrible and so difficult to comprehend. Modern commentators have more or less exonerated the British government from the charge of genocide so freely laid by partisan commentators from the time of John Mitchel on. Contemporary economic doctrines, political decisions about the extent and nature of relief, the concatenation of recurring blight, the difficulties of communications – all played their part. The government ministers responsible who seemed so unsympathetic to the stricken were just as callous, mean and self-righteous in dealing with the poor and needy in Britain at the time. The landlord class must take some responsibility and there were those who saw it as a Malthusian judgement on the feckless, over-fertile Irish peasant.

Ireland was changed utterly by the visitation. The days of relentless sub-division of land and early marriage were gone. Primogeniture ruled and younger sons and daughters left to preserve the integrity of family holdings. The Irish at home found a new and deeper hatred of their landlords, who with rare exceptions rack-rented and evicted with extra fervour in the Famine years, and they were more than willing to take part in the land agitation which followed a few decades later. The most effective relief was provided by private agencies, notably the Society of Friends, who laboured to alleviate the hunger and disease where they were greatest. Several Protestant agencies were accused with some justice of 'souperism' – offering food in exchange for conversion – and, though most who conformed to save their lives quickly reverted when the threat was over, the charge, like that of genocide, lived on to assume mythic proportions especially among emigrants. One notable philanthropist, Vere Foster, who was based in Belfast, used much of his personal fortune to aid emigration. When news came of the death rate in the Famine ships he took passage himself to experience the conditions. His resulting agitation in Britain and America caused such an outcry that the Board of Trade laid down minimum standards for the transport of travellers. Those who survived the 'coffin' ships of the 1840s established an Ireland of diaspora with a population in 1890 of three million Irish-born who lived abroad.

These endured hardship and social despisal for many years until they established their own only partly-assimilated communities in New York, Boston and Chicago. Wherever Irish communities were established, whether in America, Australia, Britain or New Zealand, they built churches and maintained Catholic schools which were staffed in many cases by Irish religious. The second half of the century saw a reformed Church with a recovered missionary zeal. Many religious brothers and sisters were recruited in Ireland and even today the number of serving religious in Irish orders abroad is much greater than at home. The emigrants preserved a sentimental vision of the old country tempered with an understandable if misdirected hatred of Britain (translated as a loathing of things 'English') which was to have a considerable effect not only on the politics of their new homes but in their reactions to affairs in Ireland.

In practice many Famine refugees landed in Canada because passages to Halifax and other north-east coast ports were much cheaper than to the US, and Canada became a back door to the States. Protestants, however, very often stayed in Canada, making Toronto as 'Irish' as Boston, but in a subtly different way. Scottish emigration to the loyal dominion had been regular and increased dramatically because of the highland clearances that followed in the century after the defeat of the Jacobites in 1746 at Culloden. As ever the Ulster Protestants found a greater harmony of settlement with their Scots kin. To a lesser extent than the Catholics in the US they preserved their Ulster ways. Each July celebration of the anniversary of the Boyne has Canadian delegates and several bands.

Emigration to America continued steadily until the 1920s and the regular stream of Irish making more or less permanent homes in England did not slacken until the Second World War. Even in the 1950s, when emigration to Britain from the Republic was considered a national scandal, the leaching from the western counties of Northern Ireland where unemployment was highest was just as serious. A country as small as Ireland and one as poor in industrial resources must expect to slough off excess population and in the century from 1840 most European countries sent people to find new lives in the lands of opportunity. Yet the numbers who left Ireland because of the condition of the distressful country was strikingly abnormal. The legacy of the 'Hungry Forties' darkens the Irish psyche still and no amount of rationalisation can fully excise the trauma.

13

LINEN MILLS AND SHIPYARDS
THE INDUSTRIALISATION OF THE PROVINCE

The creation of the industrial region of the Lagan valley was one of two significant features of Ulster history in the second half of the nineteenth century. The other was the adamant resistance by unionists to what came to be called Home Rule. The two features are linked and to the prosperous industrialists and their Protestant employees the second was seen as containing the seeds of dissolution of the first. Catholics were employed in the factories and on Dargan's Island but rarely in positions of authority and, at the regularly recurring occasions of sectarian tension, in some physical danger.

Ulster had little in the way of natural resources and was dependent on Britain not only for fuel and raw materials but also for markets. In a very real sense Ulster, at least the Protestant east, was part of the United Kingdom; the Act of Union had worked there if in no other part of Ireland. It seemed to assimilate the spirit of the industrial revolution which made Britain a world leader as if by some kind of economic osmosis.

The instinct to centralise and modernise was at work from well before the end of the previous century. The fifty-year career of the Belfast cotton industry was a kind of rehearsal for the more enduring linen trade which successfully, from an economic if not a human perspective, made the transition from cottage to factory. After Lancashire's 'King Cotton' successes had by the 1830s effectively killed the Ulster trade, the factories became linen mills. By 1900 there were more than three-quarters of a million spindles and 30,000 power looms in operation in the city of Belfast and its near vicinity. In a classic pattern, engineering, which had come into existence as a maintenance ancillary for the mills, became an industry on its own with a rich export trade and a worldwide reputation for quality.

Also experienced was a phenomenon observable in prosperous industrial regions throughout the world: success was independent of the original stimulus to the siting of the industry in a particular region. It depended more upon reputation and the entrepreneurial ability of the masters. Just as Sheffield's preeminence in cutlery was based not upon its original access to steel and the grinding powers of the local stone, so Ulster's shipyards, foundries, ropeworks, linen mills, bacon-curers, tobacco factories and aerated water distilleries, the products of which made her name internationally famous, survived and prospered without native coal and with much importing even of flax.

This association of excellence of product with place may be seen in the experience of the Derry shirt trade. It was begun by William Scott in a very small way in the 1830s to satisfy the new fashion for lighter shirts of cotton with linen facings which were replacing the older flannel models. It began as a family business with the men doing the weaving and the women the design and make-up. Scott travelled to Glasgow to push his wares and soon had a full order book. The business expanded and so began the practice of domestic contract work, with the material being distributed by overseers to out-workers who returned the finished hand-sewn garments for inspection and payment.

In 1857 the Scottish partners Tillie and Henderson introduced the first sewing-machines to the city and set them up in a huge factory which still stands as an example of Victorian industrial grandeur. (It had the distinction of being mentioned in Marx's *Das Kapital*.) Further factories nearly as large were built by Hogg and McIntyre, Hogg and Mitchell, Welch Margetson and others, and by the beginning of World War I, the industry's golden age, there were 38 firms which employed 18,000 factory hands and used 80,000 outworkers. When the Northern Ireland state was set up, Derry lost its Donegal hinterland and became an unemployment black spot. Yet in spite of the coming of man-made fibres the city's shirt factories continued to give employment to women. A second boom came with the 1939–45 war but by the 1960s the import of cheaply made shirts from the Far East diminished the native trade and though it continues to some extent the glory days are gone. Amateur sociologists used to speculate about the nature of life in a city where there was virtually full employment for women and practically none for men but no formal investigations were conducted nor conclusions drawn.

Scott was unusual as a pioneer in that he was native. The great names: the Ritchie Brothers who began to build ships on the Lagan; Harland and Wolff who fifty years later made the industry world-famous with their yards on the island in Belfast Lough that had been artificially created by William Dargan's railroads; George Smith Clark who founded the rival firm of Clark and Workman – none were Irish but they accepted the union as a fact, most lending their active support to conservative politics and favouring the Orange Order. (Just before the foundation of the new state in 1920, Clark led the agitation for the sacking of all Catholics working in the shipyards and other heavy industries.)

The real inventive genius of Ulster shipbuilding, William Pirrie, was native in blood, born in Quebec of Ulster parents, and brought home to County Down on the death of his father. Starting as an apprentice in Harland and Wolff he quickly became chief draughtsman and by 1880 was the most powerful man in the company, becoming chairman in 1895. The *Oceanic,* built for the White Star Line and launched in 1899, was, at 17,274 tons, the largest ship in the world. The reputation of the firm continued to rise in the new century with the launch of the *Olympic* in 1910 but the loss of the *Titanic* on her maiden voyage on 14 April 1912 was a setback both financially and symbolically for firm and city. Pirrie was essentially liberal and pragmatic in his approach to Ulster life. He supported Home Rule politically but remained a unionist in economic terms. By the time he died in 1924 (appropriately on board a luxury liner) he had accepted the state of Northern Ireland as the best of a bad job.

Derry, too, had its shipbuilding hour thanks to the

entrepreneurial and technical skills of William Coppin who, hailing from Kinsale, built both sailing and steam ships at Pennyburn on the west bank of Rosses Bay on the Foyle. His steamships were not a commercial success, though when the *Great Northern* (a rival's tribute to Brunel's *Great Western*) put to sea in 1843 she was the world's largest screw-propelled ship. The Derry yard was worked by W. F. Biggar in the decade from 1882 to 1892 and by Swan Hunter of Tyneside for a further period from 1912 till 1924 when the depression, both international and local, dealt a final blow. The harbour's graving dock was to prove extremely useful to the Allied forces during the Battle of the Atlantic in World War II.

It is important to say that though there were and are exceptions to the general equations: Protestant = Unionist and Catholic = Nationalist, they are sufficiently true not to require that qualification. There were Catholic unionists who felt that their careers and businesses prospered because of the links with Britain, and enough of an old Presbyterian radicalism persisted to produce some Protestant Home Rulers. These included J. G. Biggar, Parnell's chief lieutenant and deviser of the procedural campaign that gave the Irish parliamentary party such power; the liberal journalists (and 'Inst' schoolfellows) James Winder Good and Robert Lynd; Paul Henry, the landscape painter and his academic brother, Robert M., professor of Latin at Queen's College; the poet and editor, Alice Milligan; Bulmer Hobson, one of the founders of Sinn Féin and an office-bearer in the revived IRB; and Roger Casement, who was executed in 1916 though he had tried to prevent the Easter Rising.

In July of 1849, when most of Ireland lay shattered by the effects of the 'Hungry Forties', the Belfast city fathers had sufficient steel and confidence to celebrate the opening of the Victoria Channel which enabled large vessels to reach the city docks at any stage of the tide, and when the queen and her consort visited the city a month later there was no atmosphere of gloom but great gaiety and rejoicing when Dargan's Island was rechristened by the name it still bears, Queen's Island. This capacity for getting on with the job was called 'northern iron' by another of Ulster's Protestant home rulers, Canon James O. Hannay, who wrote many novels as 'George A. Birmingham'. The Protestant marchers whose triumphalism led to sometimes murderous riots were often sterling workmates and, though when the whistles sounded to mark the end of a day's work in yard or mill they walked to homes in different parts of the black city from their Catholic mates, they would have been individually certain of warm and generous hospitality had they visited each other's slum dwellings.

Once the terrors of hunger and disease were past, rural Ulster settled down to if not prosperity at least to frugal comfort and general amity between the two traditions. Town police were still seen with some justice as partisan but the Royal Irish Constabulary which policed most of Ulster was respected as even-handed. Ulster's reputation as the heart and lungs of industrial Ireland obscured the fact that the greater part of its population lived in small towns or in the country. Here much more than in the two cities the politically opposed communities depended upon each other's labour. Intermarriage was not uncommon though the practice was discouraged by the post-Famine Catholic Church, which shared more than a little in the prosperity that characterised the quarter-century from 1850 on. Ironically it was while Ulster Catholics were clearly underprivileged, in general poor, uneducated and 'greatly inferior', that they seemed less of a threat both to the Protestants (whom they equalled in total numbers but not in employment, wealth or influence) and to the union upon which the province's remarkable progress clearly depended. Once real prosperity seemed possible, and the splendid cathedrals in Monaghan, Armagh, Derry and Letterkenny appeared to indicate this, though some took an unconscionable time a-building, tocsins began to sound in Protestant minds.

The main nineteenth-century political movements such as Young Ireland and Fenianism which so affected the rest of Ireland had only a muted effect in the north. Charles Gavan Duffy, one of the original founders and editor of the *Nation,* was a Cavan man and in 1850 he made an early move in the rural agitation that was the forerunner of the Land League. His Tenant League he called rather optimistically 'a league of north and south', which nobody doubted meant a league of Protestant and Catholic. The aims were the 'three Fs' – fair rent, fixity of tenure and freedom of sale (a rural equivalent of the modern 'key money' and meant to compensate the relinquishing tenant for improvements made). The deleterious practice of increasing rents after such improvements had been one of the just pre-Famine grievances of the frugal tenant and had the effect of actually decreasing the value of his property to the landlord. There were several Tenant League meetings in Ulster including one held in Ballybay in October, that were noted more for cosy rhetoric than the formulating of plans. One reason for its short-term failure in Ulster was Protestant self-consciousness at leaguing with Catholics; the other was that in the 'Ulster Custom' a version of the three Fs was common practice, though when an emancipationist County Down landlord, Sharman Crawford, tried to give an unshakable legal basis to the 'custom' in 1847 his bill was heavily defeated. It was not until 1870 and Gladstone's first land act that the practice became law.

Ulster was spared the main disruptions both of Fenianism in the 1860s and the 'Land War' (1879–82). There were undoubtedly some Ulster cells and a general if unspecific support for 'action' among some Catholics. The IRB also provided Protestants with 'Fenian' as a new pejorative name for Catholics to add to 'Taig' and 'Papish'. Though the Fenian uprising in 1867 was mismanaged and risible the movement had a profound effect upon Irish and English affairs. Gladstone took its existence as a symptom of deep-rooted disaffection in Ireland with the union and lent all his powers to 'pacify' the country. He had some awareness of what the Ulster reaction to that mission might be, probably more than Parnell, but he, like all the liberals, did not understand what 'loyalism' meant to the Protestant north. Only the Conservatives had an inkling that it could mean fighting a war against Great Britain and its monarch to prove its 'loyalty' to them. Something of this determination began to be seen during the Land League agitation when some landlords took it upon themselves to form vigilante bands against possible outrages and reserved the right to 'drill' them. The crops in the charge of the beleaguered Captain Boycott were harvested by fifty armed Orangemen from Cavan and Monaghan under the protection of a thousand RIC officers.

Though land agitation never had the intensity that it had in other provinces, the names of two Ulster landlords (both from Donegal) achieved demonic status. In 1861 John George Adair, a successful land speculator who had become possessed of the central Donegal estates of Glenveagh, Derryveagh and Gartan, used the excuse of the murder of his steward James Murray to clear all the tenants from these lands. The place is one of startling beauty and Adair intended to make the glen into a deerpark and live in Scottish baronial splendour in the loughside castle which he completed in 1870. The estate was bought in 1937 by Henry McIlhenny, the descendant of one of those evicted, and it is now a national park. The other was William Clements, Lord Leitrim, who filled the role of pitiless Irish landlord to perfection. Evictions, *droit de seigneur*, enclosures were the characteristics of his rule in north Donegal. He tried to destroy the Ulster Custom, made legal in 1870, and was the most cordially hated man in Ireland, shunned even by his fellow landlords. Several attempts were made on his life before he was wounded and then clubbed to death on 2 April 1878 near Cratlagh Wood west of Milford. In spite of reward money that topped £10,000 no one was arrested for his murder or that of his clerk and driver. It seems clear that even the police, who knew the assailants, did not over-exert themselves to find convincing evidence.

The end of landlordism in Ireland was achieved elsewhere but Ulster benefited from the land acts of 1880, 1885, 1887, 1891 and 1903 which brought tenant purchase within the reach of all leaseholders. When Gladstone felt with some justification that he had successfully started the process that would finally settle the land question he turned his attention to the other Irish question, Home Rule. This was to prove rather more elusive.

14

'ULSTER WILL FIGHT!'
THE SOLEMN LEAGUE AND COVENANT

The famous (or infamous) battle cry (or rabble-rouser) – the distinction defines the commentator's politics – was uttered by Lord Randolph Churchill on 22 February 1886 as he landed at Larne from the Stranraer steamer after a characteristically rough crossing. He prefixed it with the ominous sentence: 'Ulster at the proper moment will resort to its supreme arbitrament of force.' It was six days after his letter to Lord Justice Fitzgibbon when he talked of 'playing the Orange Card'. The stimulus to these extreme statements was the election of the previous year which returned the Liberals and was Parnell's finest hour, Home Rulers having being returned for every seat outside east Ulster.

Home Rule had been the activists' next goal after the settlement of the land question, although the movement founded in 1870 with Isaac Butt as its leader had been decorously constitutional. When the obstruction tactics devised mainly by Biggar (and anathema to Butt) were made into effective statesmanship by the brilliant young rising star, Parnell, who was first elected to parliament as member for Meath in 1875, it was clear that Butt would soon be eclipsed; his death on 5 July 1879 made the embarrassment of ousting him unnecessary. Gladstone's characteristic attitude of moral superiority may have amused and infuriated his opponents but his courage and energy were never in doubt. Home Rule was 'the fixed desire of the nation, clearly and constitutionally expressed'. It was clear that one of the most urgent pieces of business of his new government was a Government of Ireland Bill to be introduced in April 1886. Its terms were modest; it offered the kind of devolution that Craig and Carson accepted for the partitioned six counties in 1921; the powers it suggested were mainly internal and concerned taxation, police, civil service and judiciary.

Churchill and the Conservatives argued that any crack in the perfect vessel of the union might lead to its absolute destruction and ultimately weaken the British Empire, which was reaching its sun-never-setting zenith. They also insisted that any power given to what was clearly going to be a nationalist regime was a betrayal of the Ulster Protestant. The doctrine of the duality of Ireland, which was to vex politics for more than a hundred years, received then its strongest formal statement so far. One cannot exculpate Churchill from the charge of political opportunism, though one must admire the effectiveness of his tactics, which anticipated those of Carson thirty years later. The time, too, was marked by drilling, vigilante bands, calls for an oath of resistance and the beginnings of the laying up of arms dumps. Churchill's local leader was Edward Saunderson who bonded anti-Home Rule MPs into an Irish Unionist party, and they found fellowship with a new breed of British members led by Joseph Chamberlain, who had been Gladstone's lieutenant and heir apparent. The bill was defeated by thirty votes on 8 June, Gladstone having been deserted by both the wings of his party. Three days later the maverick Orange MP William Johnston wrote in his diary, 'We decided to stop drilling for the present.'

There was some celebration in Protestant Belfast but it was muted because the city was in the grip of the most severe rioting of the century which had started four days earlier. Churchill had long ago left to celebrate the coming defeat of Gladstone's administration and the detonator which set off the disturbances is thought to have been the triumphalist remark of a Catholic in the shipyards. Yet Churchill and his Ulster confederates must take some blame for preparing the charges. The fighting, which was concentrated mainly in the poorer streets close to the city centre, lasted intermittently until September and the official death toll was put at thirty-two dead and 377 injured, though the actual number of fatalities was nearer fifty. Ulster Protestants truly believed that Home Rule apart from being 'Rome Rule' meant an end to prosperity. They saw themselves as a future persecuted minority and took great comfort in the sense of being an embattled and gallant few, a return to the mentality that had so sustained their forefathers on the walls of Derry. They may have had some tolerance if little psychological under-standing of their decent Catholic for fellow-Ulstermen, but they had no such respect for those in the other three provinces who in their eyes were dirty, feckless, and incapable of self-government. Salisbury, who led the Conservative and Unionist government that followed Gladstone's, had summed up the Protestant view when he said at a meeting in London: 'You would not confide free representative institutions to the

Hottentots, for example . . . '

Gladstone tried again in 1893 and though his majority was small the bill scraped through, only to be thrown out by the Lords. The bill offered a more phased introduction of the 1886 terms but since Parnell was dead, and Parnellism nearly so, the defeat added little to the disarray. The bill was lost in September but already Belfast had signalled its disapproval with riots and a march-past of the Linen Hall by 100,000 loyalists watched from the platform by Arthur Balfour, who had been Irish chief secretary and was within ten years to be a Conservative prime minister. It was the defeat of Balfour's government in 1905 and the Liberal successes in the general election in 1906 that brought the question of Home Rule into sharp focus again.

The intervening years were politically calm but they saw Irish energies diverted into alternative activities, mostly cultural, though with a strong nationalist flavour. The Gaelic League, founded in 1893 by Douglas Hyde, a Connacht Protestant, and Eoin MacNeill, a Catholic from Glenarm, County Antrim, was the latest and the most successful of a series of initiatives designed to save the Irish language from extinction. The league's activities, which had a strongly self-conscious element of adult education combined with entertainment, changed the life of town and country alike. The store of Gaelic culture was recovered from its cobwebby vaults and Irish music and song, dancing and literature experienced a renaissance as striking as that associated with Yeats, Lady Gregory and J. M. Synge. The two movements were, in fact, complementary, for Hyde and Lady Gregory had become conscious of the hidden culture in much the same way. As Yeats put it, Hyde learned his Irish from 'the company of old countrymen' and many of the early Abbey plays must be seen as generated by collaboration rather than by individual authors.

League organisation was extremely efficient and the branches countrywide provided a network which was later to have considerable political, not to say revolutionary, significance. The league attracted a number of Protestants, who saw it as a means of national commitment without the peril of political activism. Hyde himself relinquished his control after twenty years when he saw that the league had become a much more politicised organisation than the one he had helped to found, though he must have realised that his famous speech 'On the necessity for de-Anglicising the Irish People' delivered on 25 November 1892 in the Leinster Hall in Dublin was essentially separatist. Ulster had about 100,000 Gaelic speakers in pockets in the Sperrins, Monaghan, Cavan, the Mournes and the Antrim Glens, and nearly 70,000 in Donegal. The Donegal *gaeltacht* provided many of the *timirí* (organisers) and *múinteoirí taistil* (travelling teachers) but League enthusiasm was confined to predictable areas, mainly in the west and south of the province and in the nationalist areas of the cities. Alice Milligan, the Omagh Protestant who with her friend Anna Johnston ran the journal *The Shan Van Vocht*, was the league's chief northern organiser. She wrote a poem in praise of the travelling teachers called 'The Man on the Wheel' and her play *The Last Feast of the Fianna* was one of the first to be staged by the Irish Literary Theatre, the precursor of the more famous Abbey.

The Gaelic League and the Gaelic Athletic Association (founded in 1884) were potent means of establishing a nationalist identity in a people for centuries dismissed as an underclass. Bulmer Hobson, who joined the league and the GAA in 1901, understood well their political potential. He and Denis McCullough breathed new life into the IRB which after more than thirty years of inaction was in considerable disarray. They created the Dungannon Club in 1905 (evoking memories of the Volunteers' assembly in 1782) which was merged with Arthur Griffith's new passively resistant and totally separatist Sinn Féin in 1907. The club 'set itself the task of uniting Protestant and Catholic Irishmen to achieve the independence of Ireland'. They published a weekly journal *The Republic* which lasted for just over six months. It was written largely by Robert Lynd who, though the son of the Presbyterian minister who had been called to Cooke's May Street church, had been a follower of James Connolly and so much of a Gaelic Leaguer in London that he became an Irish teacher. The very trenchant political cartoons were by the four Morrow brothers, one of whom later became art editor of *Punch*, though Lynd did the most famous, called 'John Bull's Famous Circus' with the ringmaster offering such attractions as *Devolution* – A Farce, Birrell's 'Comic Clowning' and Redmond's 'Sleight of Hand'. It was clear that Sinn Féin and the IRB were in no mood to settle for the diluted Home Rule that John Redmond, as Parnell's heir, was prepared to accept.

The Liberal administration of 1906 is famous in history for showing the first measures of what was later to become the welfare state. It had crushed the opposition so decisively that it had no need of Irish support. Its Irish Council bill was described by Campbell-Bannerman, the prime minister, as 'a little, modest, shy, humble effort'. It was repudiated even by the Redmondites but set the Ulster Unionists' temperature soaring again. Asquith, who became prime minister in 1908, hoped for a gradualist approach to the final settling of the Irish question. His 'wait and see' was a gift to political enemies and cartoonists alike, and it must be said that like the rest of his government, his prime concern was not Ireland but his welfare policy and a need to weaken the power of the House of Lords. The destruction by the upper house of Lloyd George's 'People's Budget' in 1910 brought the constitutional crisis to a head. Asquith went to the country twice and the Liberals were returned with so depleted a majority that they were again dependent upon nationalist support.

To the Ulster Protestants, now with a stolid but very efficient leader in James Craig, it was clear that the power of the Lords would be so reduced that it could no longer block the passage of a Home Rule bill and it was even more manifest that Redmond would get a bill introduced as a matter of urgency. The Unionists were as ever bristling with old fears and armed with the spectre of Pius X's *Ne Temere* decree of 1908 and its application in the notorious McCann case in 1910, when a Catholic Belfast man married to a Protestant left his wife and took his childen with him with the church's public approval. They began to prepare for resistance. Major Crawford, a veteran of the Boer War, was put in charge of buying arms. Drilling commenced again, with Orange lodges as the basis for organisation, and the brilliant Dubliner, Sir Edward Carson, threw in his lot with the beleaguered brothers in the northeast. He differed from Craig in that he was a passionate believer in the union whereas the Ulsterman was prepared to settle for partition. But they worked together very well. The Liberal administration both feared and dismissed the possibility of Ulster resistance. They always had less ability than the Conservatives in dealing firmly with the northern Unionists and they shared with the southern nationalists a euphoric belief that a few nights of rioting in Belfast and and Derry and some attacks on isolated Catholic farms would be the only adverse reactions to the bill.

Balfour, whose honeymoon with Ulster had been short-lived, was replaced by Bonar Law as head of the Conservative and Unionist party in 1911. He dearly wanted to return to power and felt that opposition to Home Rule alone would provide that. Like Chamberlain he felt that devolution would inexorably destroy the empire and the *Pax Britannica* that was the envy of the rest of the world. He joined Carson and Craig on platforms and promised unspecified help if the loyalists were placed in the position of 'holding the pass'. The Third Home Rule bill was introduced on 11 April 1912, proposing much the same terms as Gladstone's 1886 bill. It was met by loud and vigorous opposition in Ulster. 28 September 1912 was designated Ulster Day and 218,000 men and women pledged themselves in a solemn league and covenant 'to use all means to defeat the present conspiracy to set up a Home Rule parliament in Ireland . . . and to refuse to recognise its authority'.

The bill was passed in the Commons on 16 January 1913 and thrown out by the Lords, passed again by the Commons on 7 July and again dismissed by the upper house. By now the Ulster Volunteer Force was well established and by September a provisional government with a military hierarchy was in existence and plans for a coup were firmly laid. In April 1914 large quantities of arms, including 35,000 rifles and 2,500,000 rounds of ammunition, were landed openly at Larne, Bangor and Donaghadee. The lesson was not lost on Hobson, MacNeill and other nationalists including Patrick Pearse who had formed a southern equivalent of the UVF at a meeting at the Rotunda Rink on 25 November the previous year. They arranged for a shipment of arms, minuscule compared with that of the UVF, which was landed at Howth on 26 July. A ban on the importation of all arms into Ireland had been made on 4 December 1913: in stark contrast to the aftermath of the Ulster gun-running, troops were sent to confiscate the guns and in a confrontation at Bachelor's Walk four people were killed and thirty-seven wounded. This move was seen as confirming the nationalist fears that the army might be turned on the Irish Volunteers but that they would never proceed against the armed north. The so-called 'Curragh Mutiny' of 20 March 1914, when General Gough persuaded fifty-seven out of seventy officers to resign their commissions rather than be used to enforce

Home Rule in Ulster, had shown that a Liberal War Office had lost control of the army. It was generally believed that the UVF through Carson had been advised by members of the High Command and he was kept informed of all War Office plans that dealt with Ulster. The perceived ability of none but a Conservative War Office to command total army obedience was to be significant later in the history of the province.

The storm was almost ready to break by the early summer but already Asquith was seeking some kind of compromise. In the circumstances, that would have to be a form of exclusion of some Ulster counties from the operation of Home Rule, for a specified period or in perpetuity. A conference summoned at Buckingham Palace in July failed to decide on an agreed form of a separate Ulster state. But all meetings were suspended and the Ulster question shelved when war broke out on 5 August. Asquith's Home Rule bill became law on 18 September but all agreed to defer its implementation until after the war, which many believed would be 'over by Christmas'. Redmond and Carson tried to outdo each other in providing recruits for the army. The home situation was defused but it was clear to all parties, constitutional or otherwise, that some form of northern state would have to be agreed before there could be peace. In fact the nature of the separate state was imposed by an impatient and ruthless Lloyd George but the war was to change Irish politics utterly.

15

SIX LOYAL COUNTIES

The war was *not* over by Christmas; the nature of the conflict
was such that no one, even as late as October 1918, would
have been so sanguine as to be confident of its being over
by *that* Christmas. Redmond, in a logical development of his
campaign for Home Rule, urged the Irish Volunteers to
enlist. In a crucial speech at a rally at Woodenbridge in
County Wicklow on 20 September 1914 he called upon
them to support the war effort, probably believing that their
duties would be local, at most national. 150,000 responded
and formed the National Volunteers but MacNeill, Hobson
and the original Rotunda founders rejected Redmond's call
and set themselves to resist conscription. The initial
enthusiasm for enlistment was soon dissipated but the anti-
British Irish Volunteers flourished. They allied themselves
with Arthur Griffith's Sinn Féin and the small but dedicated
Citizens' Army which had been formed to protect the
strikers during the 1913 general strike and formed the
nucleus of the force which rose at Easter 1916.

The Irish-born Lord Kitchener was appointed British
Secretary for War in August 1914 and, aware of the depleted
state of the 'contemptible little army', set about massive
recruiting. He turned to Carson, although the two men
could not abide each other, and asked for the Ulster
Volunteers. Carson and Craig immediately delivered thirty-

five thousand men who were to form the 36th (Ulster) division. Craig became quarter-master general and Carson served in various posts in the war administration, including Attorney-General and First Lord of the Admiralty, but he resigned from the cabinet in January 1918 on discovering that Lloyd George was working on an all-Ireland Home Rule bill. The division fought magnificently at the Ancre, the tributary of the Somme, in July 1916, some wearing Orange insignia. The stance was deliberately in contrast to the actions of the 'back-stabbers' of the Dublin Easter Rising six weeks earlier. Five and a half thousand of the Ulster division were killed on the first two days of the offensive. It must be said that their Catholic Irish brothers fought just as hard and with casualties just as severe, in other salients, including the ill-fated Gallipoli expedition. When the final fatality lists were computed it was clear that death was not sectarian. Of about 50,000 Irish who died in the war half, at least, were Catholic. Many of the survivors returned home to take up opposing positions in Sinn Féin and the UVF.

The war, as ever, caused an economic boom. After a short initial slump in the shipyards in 1914 orders flowed in. In 1918 alone Harland and Wolff launched over 200,000 tons of merchant shipping; Workman Clark (formerly Clark and Workman), concentrating on fighting ships, built a quarter of a million tons. Other industries shared in the prosperity. Belfast produced half of the Royal Navy's rope supplies, Derry shirt output reached new heights and Pirrie began to build planes. Harry Ferguson, Ireland's first plane-maker (and an active UVF gunrunner), revolutionised food production by his invention of an all-purpose farming mechanism which he mounted on one of his own tractors. It was a time, too, of rare domestic peace, so that the Easter Rising made comparatively little impact. It was not until the protracted executions of the signatories of the 1916 proclamation that the terrible beauty spawned terrible anger. Lloyd George's bill to apply conscription to Ireland, which he introduced in April 1918, was fiercely resisted, but more ominous was his arrogation of the right to settle the Irish question by imposed partition. Most realists had accepted that some such imposition was better than a civil war in which Catholics, almost totally without arms, would be no match for the UVF and the partisan British army. Even Joe Devlin, for many years the leader of northern nationalists and Redmond's Ulster counterpart, had come to accept it.

The war ended in November 1918 and in Winston Churchill's famous words, delivered in the House of Commons in 1922, in spite of a world deluge, '. . . as the waters fall short, we see the dreary steeples of Fermanagh and Tyrone emerging once again.' In the election of 1918 Sinn Féin won seventy-three of 105 Irish seats. (The name was taken from Griffith's separatist pre-war movement and it was the political arm of the IRA.) They constituted themselves Dáil Éireann, effectively declared themselves independent of Britain and assumed authority over all Ireland. The war of Irish independence had begun and the Protestant north prepared itself for a civil war. There were some IRA incidents, including the capture on 14 February

1920 of Shantonagh RIC barracks in Monaghan and sporadic activity in Tyrone and Donegal.

By now Lloyd George had published his Government of Ireland Bill (passed 20 December 1920) granting devolved parliaments in Ulster and in Dublin. He had tried to get the Unionists to accept the historical nine-county province which, with its roughly equal religious balance, would predispose to eventual reunification, but they would settle for nothing but the safe counties of Antrim, Down, Armagh and Derry with Tyrone and Fermanagh lumped in to make the new state viable. They were determined to hold a workable territory where Unionist supremacy would be permanent and inviolable and they were aided in this by such efficient civil servants as Sir Ernest Clark, who as Under-Secretary of Ulster saw the safe delivery of 'Northern Ireland', as much a misnomer as Ulster, and equally unacceptable to the permanent nationalist one-third minority. The *fait accompli* may have shaken Irish nationalists outside the north but their attentions were held elsewhere. With the same kind of euphoric dismissal that had characterised attitudes to Ulster Protestants since the time of Parnell and Gladstone's first Home Rule bill, they assumed (as Asquith had earlier) that the Six Counties, as nationalists took pains to call the statelet, would prove economically, if not morally, unmanageable.

The year of the progress of the Government of Ireland Bill through parliament was characterised by the inevitable Ulster response to heightened political activity: sectarian violence. In January the municipal election in Derry produced a narrow majority for a Sinn Féin-Nationalist alliance over the Unionists: twenty-one to twenty. Derry Catholics with a population majority of 5,000 were able to elect their first Catholic mayor, H. C. O'Doherty. The victory was made possible by the introduction of a proportional representation system of voting and even the Unionists, masters of ward-boundary manipulation, could do nothing about it. (The speedy ending of PR for local government elections by the new Minister of Home Affairs, Dawson Bates, in 1922, gave Derry Unionist mayors until 1968, when a development commission replaced the city corporation.) A period of comparative peace in the city ended with rioting in April when some republican prisoners were brought to the city jail in Bishop Street, a thoroughfare which acted as a kind of neutral boundary between the Catholic Bogside and the Protestant Fountain. Trouble continued for some weeks, flaring into a gun-battle between the local IRA and the RIC and resulting in the death of the head of the Special Branch. The UVF had been resurrected and all the ingredients for a summer of confrontation and carnage were present. The illegal force had no difficulty in making accommodation with the army and police, though several Catholic officers resigned at the evidence of the partiality.

In all, fifty people died in the 'Riots', as the events of that spring and summer were afterwards known. (As proof of the persistence of normal instincts even in times of terror it was noticed that the usual Sunday evening *paseo* of young men and women which normally moved through the town, across the Craigavon Bridge and out the Prehen Road took place on the black Sunday of 20 June on a different, safer road.) After that troubled summer Derry was quiet. The local IRA virtually ceased to operate and anti-partitionism passed into the hands of the local clergy. The UVF eventually received government sanction on 1 November 1920 as members of one of three special constabularies which were formed to 'keep the peace'. The most significant of these were 'B'-Specials, who were unpaid part-timers with local UVF officers as commanders, and that constabulary persisted as a feared anti-Catholic force of dubious reputation until its disbandment in 1970. The Fermanagh commander, Basil Brooke, had been a prominent Ulster player in the Curragh 'mutiny' and became prime minister of Northern Ireland in 1943, proving the most unyielding Unionist in the state's history, more adamantine even than Craig.

That summer saw violence too in other parts of the north: the pattern was usually of Protestant attacks on Catholic homes and businesses with murderous intimidation in workplaces. There was some Catholic retaliation but Catholics were generally outnumbered and seriously under-armed. There were bloody scenes in Lisburn, Dromore and Banbridge but the most ferocious incidents occurred in Belfast. By the end of August 400 Catholics had been driven from their homes, a million pounds worth of damage done and twenty-three civilians had died. The passing of the Government of Ireland Act did not ameliorate the situation. For two years more the province was in the grip of sectarian violence, or more precisely anti-Catholic outrage. In 1922, 232 people died, 1,000 were seriously wounded and £3 million pounds worth of mainly Catholic property was destroyed. In one notorious incident, blamed on the B-Specials, Owen McMahon, a nationalist politician, and four of his family were killed in their home on 29 March 1922.

Eventually law and order was restored and optimists hoped for some sign of Craig's stated wish to reconcile the two communities in Northern Ireland. He was not a bigot and scrupulously honest, but he was prime minister of a party that was far from united except in its unionism. His creation of the official constabularies did give him some control over the more rabid elements among his supporters. It was this need to conciliate his right wing that had led to the appointment to Home Affairs, of Dawson Bates, a solicitor of notorious and public sectarianism. The truth was that Craig was a tired man, his health weakened by his Boer War campaigns and his time in France with the Ulster Division. Unlike the new government of young men that was cautiously licking itself into shape in Dublin, his administration was middle-aged and mediocre. Only he had the vision to realise that for the survival of the state which he had gone to Herculean lengths to achieve, the one-third of the population which had been included, with few exceptions, against its will had to be reconciled. Yet through fatigue and inertia he allowed gerrymandering and other nefarious means of Unionist dominance to continue. He insisted the Northern Ireland Civil Service commissioners reserve one-third of posts for Catholics (though that was easily got round by blocking promotion) and though the same allocation was imposed upon the new Royal Ulster Constabulary only a sixth of the places were taken up.

There was one last battle, however, that Craig had to fight. According to article 12 of the Anglo-Irish Treaty which superseded Lloyd George's original bill, a boundary commission was to be set up to determine the frontiers of Northern Ireland, 'in accordance with the wishes of the inhabitants, so far as may be compatible with economic and geographic conditions'. The article was symptomatic of the treaty delegates' unconcentrated attitude to the north, and with the convulsions of the civil war, the death of Michael Collins and the need to nurture the infant Free State, Ulster played a smaller than due part in the Dublin government's preoccupations. Craig's position was summed up in the phrase ever since associated with him, 'not an inch'. He would not cooperate with any such commission. The chairman, Justice Feetham of the South African supreme court, decided that economics and geography should override 'the wishes of the inhabitants'. Eoin MacNeill, the Free State representative, found himself outmanoeuvred. Matters came to a head when the *Morning Post* published on 7 November 1925 a map showing that the commission's report would make little difference to the existing arrangements. The resulting crisis was settled in a speedily arranged 'summit' on 3 December, attended by the three concerned prime ministers, Baldwin, Cosgrave and Craig, which confirmed the existing border. Craig returned to his northern fastness 'happy and contented'. The northern nationalists from border areas had lost out, although the Catholics in Belfast and the four eastern counties may have felt some comfort and confraternity in the long, long struggle that lay ahead.

Britain's attitude to the new state was rather that of the headmaster of a public school to the regime of the senior prefects. She had retained most of the powers that a state regards as significant and felt she could leave the internal running to the new provincial government. There were some characteristics that she would have liked the new state to have – ideally a replication of British institutions. If this proved impossible, given the task of keeping the junior common room under control, then she was not going to be too exercised; if such ideals as civil liberties and equality of opportunity irrespective of race or creed could not quite be guaranteed then she would take the prefects' word that the time was not yet ready for such privileges. Dawson Bates's Offences Against the State Act, first enacted in 1924, gave the police impressive powers of arrest and detention. It was renewed annually until 1931, when it was replaced by the even more draconian and much longer-lasting Special Powers Act.

Britain would have liked, too, to have established a non-denominational education system with the hope of a gradual *rapprochement* between the two traditions. A committee under the chairmanship of Robert Lynd (boycotted by Catholics on the instructions of their pastors) had been set up by the flamboyant Lord Londonderry, who had sacrificed a more dazzling political career at Westminster to become Craig's Minister of Education. Acting on its recommendations he tabled an education act which proposed non-denominational schools. This was greeted with such hostility by Catholics and Presbyterians alike that, though the structural proposals were left untouched, a majority of Northern Ireland schools would continue to be church-controlled in management and the teaching of religion. The question of denominational education was to recur regularly for the next fifty years and Londonderry, having had enough of the sterile politics of Northern Ireland, resigned in 1925. In essence, Northern Ireland had become not only a police state but also a confessional one with Catholic and Protestant clergy often at one in principle if not in doctrine. For too long the metaphorical headmaster remained aloof in his study, appearing only at school concerts and prize days. When the Northern Ireland state collapsed in the early 1970s because of its moral and structural flaws the headmaster was forced to dismiss the prefects and face the roaring boys in person.

The initial reaction of nationalist politicians to the new state was abstention. Their leader 'Wee Joe' Devlin had been active in politics since 1886, when at the age of fifteen he helped the Parnellite Thomas Sexton to win West Belfast. He came from the Lower Falls, the heart of riotland, and was to maintain a control and respect until his death that was almost monarchical. He could have become head of the Irish Parliamentary Party on Redmond's death but he preferred to maintain his northern base. He defeated de Valera in the Falls in 1918 and was a member of the new parliament from 1921 until his death in 1934. His sense of betrayal by the treaty terms was mitigated by a gradual determination to use his MPs and local councillors as levers for the social betterment of his generally poor people. They began to attend parliament, which met after 1932 in a splendidly over-elaborate building at Stormont, whenever 'matters apropos' were being discussed. Since the majority of Catholics wanted a united Ireland their real ambition was held to be not the bringing down of a government but the annihilation of the state. They could not, therefore, form a loyal opposition and did not merit such an opposition's powers and status. Devlin and his younger supporters felt the sterility of their position and the monumental stasis of the regime. The result was a deterioration of political organisation on the nationalist side, which provided a sad contrast to the relentlessly efficient Unionist machine. It is certain that Westminster would in the early years (when the headmaster was keeping a closer eye on the new prefects) have responded to a united and vocal opposition. Better terms as regards education could well have been secured, although as time went on it was generally conceded that in purely scholastic matters the Ministry of Education's *practice* was entirely even-handed.

Since Westminster made all the important decisions and heavily subsidised the state through the years of its existence, improvements in welfare provision in Britain, especially after 1945, were applied step by step to Northern Ireland. It was Craig (Viscount Craigavon from 1927) who insisted upon this as a principle at the very beginning. This led to a situation in the late 1950s when in such matters as health, unemployment benefits and education the Northern Ireland state was greatly in advance of the Republic (which had taken the place of the Free State in 1948). Economists were quick to conclude that the Six Counties were never going to provide a sterling example of productivity. The welfare state was needed there as in no place else under Westminster's control. The west of the province lost its hinterland of Donegal, which brought permanent depression to Derry and Strabane. The second city had, like Belfast, reached an impressive level of urban amenity by the outbreak of war in 1914 but the 1920s and even more grievously the 1930s were periods of high unemployment and associated social distress.

Working-class housing throughout the state was poor, and since such matters were in the control of local government there was open discrimination in matters of allocation. Economic conditions in these first two decades were such that there were not many public housing schemes, but in Unionist-controlled councils, a large majority, sites were chosen carefully. This was most noticeable in Derry, where a growing Catholic population had to be ward-manipulated so that the Unionist hegemony was preserved. On the west bank of the Foyle, that piece of land taken from the O'Donnells at the time of the plantation, the city had two wards grotesquely jigsawed so that the small Protestant North ward should contain as few Catholics as possible, while the huge South ward (returning the same number of councillors) was the natural home of the Catholic majority. This ward distinction was engineered even in private house sales; Protestants could always be found to offer a higher price than Catholics in the North ward or in the mainly Protestant Waterside east-bank ward. Other tactics included multiple 'business' votes, and municipal suffrage confined to householders. These devices were practised wherever necessary with an exemplary thoroughness. 'Second-class citizenship' was also maintained by sectarian appointments to posts in the public sector and by the relative paucity of Catholic employers. The Orange Order flourished as never before and its ties with the Unionist party headquarters in Glengall Street in Belfast were strong. So effective and pervasive was the government machine that even Lord Reith's BBC, 'the finest and most independent broadcasting system in the world', was not proof against it. BBC NI (begun as 2BE on 15 September 1924) was to be the scene of many wars of attrition as controllers, confidently assumed to be puppets of Glengall Street, tried to maintain a establishment-respecting or blandly neutral service.

Life among the poor in Belfast in the 1930s was as grim as in depressed industrial cities elsewhere during the world slump. There were industrial riots in 1932 which turned, as ever, into sectarian trouble with police using guns only 'in Roman Catholic areas'. In 1933 a Catholic publican called Dan O'Boyle was shot in York Street, the first victim of sectarian strife since 1922. There was trouble too in 1934 but 1935, the occasion of Protestant celebration of George V's silver jubilee, was made an excuse for what amounted to an anti-Catholic pogrom with injuries inflicted and houses burnt. Even Dawson Bates found it necessary to ban all parades from 18 June of that year. The Orange grand master in a tone of voice experienced before and since announced: 'You may be perfectly certain that on the twelfth of July Orangemen will be marching throughout Northern Ireland.' Bates withdrew the ban, Craigavon being absent on one of his ever more frequent cruises. The worst violence broke out only as the day was nearly over. An Orange procession was attacked in Royal Avenue and fierce rioting followed. When the dreary computation of damage was compiled it was found that eight Protestants and five Catholics had been killed, a large majority of the wounded were Catholics, and 2,000 Catholics had been driven from their homes. John MacNeice, the Bishop of Down and Home-Ruler father of the poet Louis MacNeice, denounced the holding of the Twelfth celebrations and the Belfast city coroner had the courage roundly to condemn the political leaders who could permit such inflammatory proceedings. The Nationalist politicians, led by the Catholic bishop, Daniel Mageean, called at Westminster for a government inquiry but Stanley Baldwin, the prime minister, characteristically washed his hands of any responsibility and said that he was constitutionally unpowered to interfere, a statement which called out for the nice 1980s' locution, 'economy of truth'.

Catholics could be as dangerous as their adversaries when roused, and some parades of the Ancient Order of Hibernians (a copycat organisation set up in 1838 to counter Orangeism and revived and turned into an effective political machine by the young Joe Devlin at the turn of the century) could be as triumphalist as any 'Twelfth' march. Yet Catholics were in general poorer, more ill-housed and socially inferior, and felt with considerable justification that most of the systems of the state were against them. In time a Catholic middle-class Belfast evolved, strangely uncertain about its political stance and on the whole conservative with a small 'c'. Catholics who lived in the border areas of the west and south were at least psychologically more serene. They tended to look socially and culturally towards Dublin and took some amusement at some of the more surrealist effects of the border: a house where the boundary line ran through the living-room; the sight of one half of Pettigo blacked-out according to Ministry of Defence war regulations while the other half, in neutral Éire (from 1936), was normally lit; and the pleasures of two-way smuggling across the eccentric and artificial frontier. This was most prevalent during the 1939–45 war, which was to be the first circumstance to breach the outer defences of the Unionists' apparently impregnable citadel.

16

THE FALL OF STORMONT

The war saved Northern Ireland from the embarrassment of being pilloried as Britain's 'hand-out region' and the object of the Treasury's increasingly vocal criticism of the cost of partition. Since the retained ports had been handed back in 1939 to neutral Éire, Lough Foyle and Derry became important as a naval base. Important also to the 'war effort' were the flatlands at Magilligan and Toome where air bases were built. The Unionists were able to flagwave to their heart's content while publicly decrying Éire's neutrality, and the general incompetence of Northern Ireland ministers and significant civic corruption were tolerated. Conscription was offered by Craigavon but declined, both actions perhaps resulting from a strong anti-conscription campaign by southern politicians and northern bishops in May 1939. About 23,000 Northern Ireland citizens joined the British forces, compared with 42,000 from the south.

Conscription apart, Northern Ireland was very much at war. It shared the high taxation (fudged as 'post-war credits'); the adaptation of its factories to the making of munitions, with an impressive output of ships (both transport and fighting), tanks and planes, and increased production in agriculture; wartime restrictions and rationing (though this hit the urban east more than the border counties). Belfast had its own blitz in 1941 with nearly a thousand fatalities, many more injuries, and severe damage to houses and the loughside shipyards and plane and factories. The fire storm which followed the incendiary raid of 15 April was fought by, among others, thirteen fire-brigades dispatched by de Valera from Dublin and the east coast towns of Dun Laoghaire, Drogheda and Dundalk. Intervention of another kind was less welcome: when Northern Ireland seemed to have become one huge transit camp for US forces in 1942 de Valera's objections were rejected by the prime minister, John Miller Andrews, saying that he had no business interfering in Northern Ireland affairs. Andrews, who had been returned unopposed for his County Down seat in every election since 1921, served from Craigavon's death on 24 November 1940 until he was ousted by the more able Basil Brooke on 1 May 1943.

Apart from the air-raids (including the dropping on 15 April 1941 of two parachute mines by a maverick German plane in Derry which killed fifteen people) Northern Ireland had a fairly quiet war. Members of the rump IRA had been interned even before the outbreak of hostilities and political activity was shelved. The 'dreary steeples of Tyrone and Fermanagh', however, did not need to emerge again for the good reason that in spite of a second world cataclysm they had kept their metaphorical high profile. The disaffected one-third of the population was as unwooed and uncooper-ative as ever but it had shared somewhat in the high employment and prosperity of the war years. The presence of the always colourful and frequently bizarre American armed forces first shocked the population out of their rather depressed provincialism and then raised their expectations. Things surely could not be the same after the war!

In the sphere of politics there was no observable change. Basil Brooke became Viscount Brookeborough in 1952 but apart from his insistence, on the occasion in 1949 of Éire's becoming a republic, that the Labour prime minister Clement Attlee declare Northern Ireland's right to remain a part of the United Kingdom for so long as the Stormont parliament wished it, no significant statesmanlike actions can be credited to him. Craigavon-like, he asked that the system of peacetime national service that began in 1949 should be applied to Northern Ireland. His request was not granted. Though the administration had no affinity with the Westminster government of the immediate post-war years Northern Ireland shared in the welfare benefits that the rest of the UK was to enjoy. Most significant of these was the Education Act of 1947 which was the equivalent of the Westminster 1944 Butler Act (and tabled at the same time). It provided for appropriate secondary education for all from the age of eleven years, though its passing caused the same kind of political and religious storm from both sides that had greeted the Londonderry Act of 1924, and led as then to the resignation of a liberal minister. The act, which offered generous third-level grants to those who wished for them, created by the 1960s a generation of young radical educated Catholics who found the Northern Ireland state as offensive as their parents did but were determined to do something about it.

The other three counties of the historical province had

not fared well since the Treaty. They were mainly rural and with the exception of the Laggan region of east Donegal not very productive. The border had the same adverse effect on their economies as on Derry and the counties of Tyrone, Fermanagh and Armagh. They endured the growing pains of the new state and were subject to the emigration drain of pre-Lemass Ireland. The Protestants who were 'caught' on the wrong side made reasonable accommodation with their Catholic neighbours, although emigration changed their communities too. This was most noticeable in Monaghan and Cavan; the Protestant farmers in Donegal seemed to be as prosperous as ever. The tradition of seasonal migration from west Donegal to Scotland continued, and as Highland hydro-electric schemes came up for contract, in many cases labour was supplied by Donegal gangers. More and more the migrants became emigrants, establishing twentieth-century Irish colonies in Glasgow and other central Scottish locations. Donegal's scenic beauty and holiday amenities earned her a growing revenue in tourism, and wartime restrictions of travel and food rationing (which persisted until the early 1950s) made the county a popular place for vacations for Ulster people of all creeds. The Gaelic revival which created summer schools in the Irish-speaking coastal areas at first for adults and then for secondary-school children played a part in arresting the economic decline of such places as Gweedore, the Rosses and Teelin. Orange processions continued to be held at various venues in these separated counties and perhaps there they had the colourful, folkloric charm claimed for them, and none of the sectarian rancour.

The twenty years from the end of the war were peaceful and, compared with the 1930s, relatively comfortable for a large majority of the population. The welfare provisions decreased the number emigrating to find work, although Catholics still were by any ideological standards an underclass. A majority of Catholics in employment were unskilled while an equivalent proportion of Protestants were skilled and had inevitably better positions. The population ratio was about 3:7 but the numbers of Catholic engineers, company secretaries, managers, registrars and university teachers were well below 10 per cent. Even Catholic doctors formed only a fifth of the medical establishment; the highest proportion was of lawyers, but at 23 per cent that fell far short of the statistical norm and may have reflected the racial love of litigation. As late as 1972, when Stormont fell, only 5 per cent of senior civil servants were Catholic.

Discrimination continued to be practised in housing allocation. By 1945, because of the stagnation of the 1930s and the destruction of so many homes in the blitz, the most plangent social need was for housing. Conditions in the working-class areas of Belfast and Derry would have disgraced Dickens's London. Poverty among the Catholic poor was measurably greater for historical reasons and because they were more likely to be unemployed. A Housing Trust was set up and local authorities were given what funds they needed to build the badly needed dwellings. Since most of the councils were Unionist-controlled (and were intended to stay that way) fairly blatant preference was given to Protestants, often with smaller families than equivalent

Catholics. It was such a piece of unwise allocation in the village of Caledon, County Tyrone, that led to the first civil rights march, the initial step in the domino-sequence which finally brought down Stormont.

It is probable that the system could not have been maintained anyway but the events of these quiet years indicate a *prima facie* case that if the Unionists had then had a statesman with the courage and the skill to make visible concessions to the minority, the history of the last quarter of the century in Northern Ireland would have been notably different. None emerged and it seemed to the ever-patient constitutional Catholics that all moves at reconciliation were being made by them, only to be rejected and mocked at the next Orange demonstration. One reason for the inertia was the lack of radical opposition. Belfast, as a large industrial city with a nineteenth-century mushroom growth like Birmingham or Liverpool, should have been a Labour stronghold. It had a large working-class population which had suffered great hardship in the pre-war years and which was granted only a slow amelioration in peacetime. Some evidence of working-class solidarity was seen in the hunger agitation of the early 1930s, but the participants, especially the Protestants, were soon recalled behind their implicit barricades. Even trades-union activity was *ad hoc* and headquarters were usually in London or Dublin. The British Labour Party did not organise there and the Northern Ireland Labour Party, though worthy, was small and at times ludicrously sabbatarian. As far as the Protestant worker was concerned, and if there were jobs going he was likely to have one, the class struggle was not vertical but lateral and the adversaries not the bosses but the feckless, lazy, manipulated and intermittently dangerous Fenians. Attempts at socialist organisation were made, especially in the years before the war, but the mass of the industrial population on both sides could be whipped in effortlessly by atavistic appeals.

The social legislation of Attlee's government was kept in place by the Conservatives under Eden and Macmillan, and Northern Ireland had equivalent security. (Sectarian reaction to the new National Health Service was confined to the Mater Hospital controversy. The board wished to preserve its Catholic ethos and the government refused all subventions.) It was noted that Catholics ambitious of a career in the civil service opted for the imperial rather than the local service. Many too, with the requisite qualifications in the Irish language, found careers in the Republic. The Nationalist party struggled manfully if vainly at Stormont and council level to represent their people's grievances, earning them the unfair soubriquet of 'green Tories'. Yet peace continued; improved social conditions seemed to have induced quietism if not content. 'Operation Harvest', the IRA campaign of the years 1956–62, was contained effectively by the RUC and the B-Specials. Security was in the hands of Brian Faulkner, one of the few Unionists with any talent for politics. He interned known members of the IRA in 1956, smarting after a successful arms raid on the virtually unguarded Gough Barracks in Armagh in 1954 and in swift response to a night of sporadic attacks on 12 December 1956. The campaign had little hope of success without the support of northern Catholics and apart from complaints about closed border roads and B-Specials' insolence at checkpoints it was largely ignored. The containment, too, was greatly assisted by de Valera's re-introduction of internment in July 1957.

In 1959 Seán Lemass, the pragmatic architect of modern Ireland, became taoiseach and without shedding a scale of his old patriotism began to prepare for a possible solution to the old question of reconciling the North that would be based on economic and social equality and mutual self-interest. By the mid-1960s he had in Stormont a man of conscience if not of great political wisdom as his opposite number. Brookeborough, Craigavon's heir, had resigned in 1963 and been replaced by Terence O'Neill, following in the tradition that while the party depended upon a proletarian vote the leaders should be drawn from the squirearchy. The 'Ulster' he inherited was changing: shipbuilding and linen manufacture, the region's pride, were hopelessly in eclipse, and something was going to have to be done about the minority, growing slowly more prosperous and containing a small but significant middle class. O'Neill was the first northern premier publicly to mention reconciliation as government policy. His choice of Brian Faulkner as Minister of Commerce was inspired, and many new industries were brought to the region. Soon multi-nationals were building plants and Northern Ireland became the leading European source of man-made fibre.

The O'Neill-Lemass meeting in January 1965 certainly broke new ground. Its purpose was non-specific but it was part of Lemass's plan for closer economic ties. O'Neill, in fact, risked less than Lemass but the older man had laid his plans carefully and had the backing of his government and the general consensus of his now buoyant country. O'Neill had not taken the same pains to bring his more awkward squad with him. His accession to the leadership had not followed upon a vote of, or even consultation with, the Unionist parliamentary party; it was rather an oligarchic gift and Brian Faulkner and other party members resented it. Even at his best O'Neill always seemed withdrawn and invincibly condescending, and he had neither the intellectual nor tactical ability successfully to conclude what he had gallantly begun. Several meetings were held during the next few years and when Jack Lynch succeeded Lemass as taoiseach, he too took pains to arrange an early meeting with the northern premier.

Grassroots Protestant reaction was swift, and old and barely latent loyalism recrudesced. The most potent anti-O'Neill force came not from within parliament but from a brilliant populist Protestant leader, Ian Paisley. Paisley began as a fundamentalist clergyman, of a type to which Ulster had become well accustomed, and which had been either execrated or adulated depending on sect. Paisleyism was vocal, vituperatively anti-Catholic and specifically anti-papal, and soon achieved an impressive if ominous following even among middle-class Protestants. In the previous century it might have been called Hannaism or Cookeism and its existence was independent of a specific charismatic leader, though one was naturally required to give it shape and drive. Paisley was a splendid example of the iconoclastic thundering latter-day Old Testament prophet: tall, vocal, tireless and fearless. He dared say the unsayable and scattered the decorous minuet of reconciliation with biblical fervour and mocking rural laughter.

The first incident that brought his name to full public awareness was his work for James Kilfedder, the Unionist candidate in West Belfast in the 1964 Westminster general election. Paisley's supporters, already a sizeable number, were involved in 1930-style riots in Divis Street. In 1966 he founded the Ulster Protestant Volunteers and a newspaper, the *Protestant Telegraph*, and from then on he was to play a constant game of harrying O'Neill and fulminating against erosion of the Protestanism of 'Ulster'. In all of this he never lost touch with the source of his power and odd divagations and minor accommodations in his career may be traced to this instinct. Anti-O'Neill graffiti appeared side-by-side with the usual recommended destination of the Holy Father. In the Protestant County Derry village of Knockloughrim at one point the message 'Lynch O'Neill' caused some semantic confusion.

O'Neill had some support, especially among middle-class and elderly Catholics, those with a stake in peace and progress, though their confidence was badly shaken two months after the meeting with Lemass when the Lockwood Committee, an entirely non-Catholic body, recommended that the promised second university should be sited not in the city of Derry where a nucleus existed in Magee College, but in the small, safe, loyal town of Coleraine. And the location of a new town, tactfully called Craigavon, only twenty-five miles from Belfast beside the banner loyalist town of Portadown caused further disenchantment. The conviction grew that the 'new Ulster' with its busy factories and full employment stopped at the Bann. It seemed that west of that defining river where Catholics were in a global majority, however strategically zoned, the old depressed Northern Ireland was going to be allowed its customary stasis. Even more ominous than the hoarse fulminations of the 'big man' was the rebirth of the UVF, which was responsible for the deaths of two Catholics in 1966 and which, to his credit, O'Neill declared illegal.

The Northern Ireland Civil Rights Association (NICRA) was founded in January 1967 and it subsumed for a time a number of reform groupings including the Dungannon-based Campaign for Social Justice, the Nationalist party which had constituted itself the official opposition after the Lemass-O'Neill meetings and a radical student group called People's Democracy which included such effective young members as Michael Farrell and Bernadette Devlin, who were to play a significant part in the fall of O'Neill. A successful NICRA march on 24 August 1968 from Coalisland to Dungannon, led by the young MP Austin Currie, protested against what was perceived as sectarian allocation of housing. It was followed by one in Derry, organised locally by the Derry Housing Action Committee (DHAC) led by Eamonn McCann and Eamonn Melaugh, and fixed for 5 October. The impetus for the Dungannon action was the allocation of a council house in the Tyrone village of Caledon (home of Earl Alexander of Tunis) to an unmarried nineteen-year-old Protestant typist. Derry was the exemplary site for a protest march; it was the Unionist icon, the Maiden City, and her virginity, as we have seen, was sedulously protected by Byzantine ward-rigging which kept a large Catholic majority from civic power.

The march was banned by William Craig, the Minister of Home Affairs, as 'provocative' and likely to clash with a hastily organised 'traditional' march by the Protestant Apprentice Boys of Derry (founded in 1814 and holding bi-annual siege celebrations of the closing of the gates in December and the relief of Derry in August). The mainly constitutional NICRA wanted to accede to Craig's ukase but the DHAC persuaded the rest to march. They were met by the usual police and B-Special 'vigour' with baton charges and an impressive panoply of anti-riot devices including water cannon. It was the kind of incident that had characterised Irish life for hundreds of years but on this occasion the news cameras of the world were there to intrude on what till then had been relatively private affairs. The rioting in Derry that night was the first serious civil disturbance to afflict the city since 1920 but it was to be repeated many times. Wilson's Labour government demanded actions and explanations and in fact NICRA's main demands were granted by October 1969. The RUC was to be reformed, the B-Specials were disbanded, Derry was to be run by a commission until reform of electoral boundaries should take place, public housing was to be administered by a non-partisan agency and safeguards against discrimination were introduced.

The cry of 'too little, too late', current at the time, now seems accurate. The historical party game of 'What if' is inherently vain but the effect such reforms might have had in, say, 1967 is incalculable. As it was, the younger and more radical elements of civil rights agitation, which included a strand of a left-wing and incipiently constitutional IRA membership, were not going to be content with what they saw as palliatives. People's Democracy saw as its main adversary not Paisleyism but O'Neill gradualism. Their 1969 Belfast-Derry march was attacked by Protestant extremists on Saturday 4 January at Burntollet and the encounter was characterised by police inaction, to put it no more strongly. There were riots in Derry that night with the usual story of police misbehaviour and the use of the now regulation anti-riot devices of CS gas and the rubber bullet. There were similar disturbances on the night of April 19 with messy police incursions into the Catholic Bogside. On 28 April O'Neill resigned, to be replaced by James Chichester-Clark, his going hastened by UVF sabotage of the Silent Valley reservoir which was blamed with some irony on the IRA. Rioting recurred in July in Dungiven, where the first death occurred, and in Belfast and Derry. The most dreaded event was the Apprentice Boys' march on 12 August. John Hume, leader of the Derry Citizens Action Committee, tried to have the march banned but failed to persuade the Home Office. The result was much worse than expectation, especially since the day had until evening been relatively quiet. The effect of the three-day 'Battle of the Bogside' was to create Free Derry, a barricade culture and the calling out of the

British army.

As if on a signal, there were old-style Protestant attacks on Catholic areas especially on the Crumlin and Falls Roads, with several deaths. The total defencelessness of the Catholic population, compared with the well-armed UVF-backed Protestants, goes a long way towards explaining their support of the Provisional IRA, which at the beginning took an old 'Defenderist' line. Figures published at the end of the month revealed ten deaths and nearly a thousand injuries, a fifth of them gunshot wounds. By then, however, the Downing Street Declaration had committed Stormont to the implementation of British standards of justice (a phrase which was to have a hollow ring to Irish ears later).

For a time the army personnel were fêted as saviours by Catholics in Derry and Belfast. The forces of moderation seemed in control. The Social Democratic and Labour Party (SDLP) was founded in August 1970 under the leadership of Gerry Fitt, who had been an MP for many years. Its main aim was the securing of a united Ireland by consent. Earlier in the year the founding of the Alliance Party, containing moderate Unionists and Catholics who were prepared to defer the SDLP's main aim to a time in the remote future, gave some hope of a Northern Ireland administration that might be even-handed and viable. Reforms were on the way but implementation was agonisingly slow and every mention of change was greeted by cries of 'sell-out' by the increasingly vocal Unionist right-wing. The Westminster general election in June returned a Conservative government with Edward Heath as prime minister and saw the introduction to the

Palace of Westminster of Ian Paisley as MP for North Antrim. With the end of Wilson's Labour administration the Unionists felt they could be more themselves. Chichester-Clark resigned in March 1971, to be replaced by Brian Faulkner. By then the moderates had lost out. They included some Protestants but the majority were Catholics, mostly middle-class though not without rural and small town support except in such traditionally republican areas as south Armagh. Faulkner suffered less hounding from Paisley who, presumably relishing the parliamentary experience, founded the Democratic Unionist Party (DUP) on 14 September. Five days before, the death of a fourteen-year-old girl in the Bogside had brought the casualty list of the Troubles to 100.

The army honeymoon had not lasted long. Soldiers were not trained as policemen and handling of small local disturbances had been inept. It was felt by the Catholic community that soldiers listened much more to the majority, that the officers would have much more in common with the establishment. The honeymoon ended with the policy of house searches (more than 17,000 in 1971) and the beginning of the IRA's active campaign. The organisation had been dubbed 'I Run Away' by the desperate Catholics in August 1969 but since then it had regrouped and a splinter faction called 'provisional', which soon became a majority, decided that the time for the resurrection of the 'armed struggle' was at hand. The first military casualty was Gunner Curtis, who was shot in Belfast on 6 February 1971. There followed years of shooting and bombing, the Provos, as they came to be called, prisoners of their own rhetoric. For some time every move by the authorities seemed designed to give them moral victories and act as a recruiting drive. Faulkner, who was more astute than the usual establishment politician, had the fatal flaw of self-esteem and decided that internment, which he had used so effectively in the 1950s, would work again. Against army advice, 342 people (nearly all Catholics) were arrested in the late summer of 1971 and grossly mistreated, while Protestant extremists, who were mainly responsible for the crisis, were left free. The disturbances which followed were terrifying in their violence. Civil unrest continued throughout the autumn and winter and reached a grisly climax on 30 January 1972 with the killing by an undisciplined force of paratroopers of thirteen unarmed civilians demonstrating against internment in Derry.

Many Catholics, mainly young people, flocked to join the Provos, and an incensed crowd in Dublin burned down the British Embassy. A tribunal of enquiry chaired by Lord Widgery exonerated the paras, to the surprise of very few Catholics, and laid the blame for the fatalities on NICRA for organising the demonstration. It was 'Bloody Sunday', as it was immediately dubbed, that spelled the end for Stormont. It was clear that Faulkner, for all his business acumen and political astuteness, could not hope to continue to rule the disaffected statelet. The parliament of Northern Ireland was dissolved on 20 March 1972, fifty-two years after its establishment. The prorogation was initially for a year, and direct rule with a new cabinet post of Secretary of State for Northern Ireland was introduced on 1 April. The Northern Ireland Constitution Act (passed on 18 April

1973) finally abolished Craigavon's and Carson's edifice. The inclusion of the one-third portion of almost entirely unwilling Catholics which was meant to give the state moral and economic ballast had in the end brought it down since no attempt was ever made at necessary reconciliation: a shotgun marriage when the girl is not even pregnant is 'but two months victuall'd'.

17

WAR AND PEACE?

The fall of Stormont did nothing to reduce violence. Apart from periods of heightened tension like the 1981 hunger strikes and IRA 'spectaculars', such as the blowing up of eighteen soldiers at Warrenpoint on 27 August 1979 (the same day that Earl Mountbatten was killed in his boat off Mullaghmore with one elderly lady and two teenagers), the deaths of eight British soldiers in a landmine attack on their bus near Ballygawley on 20 August 1988 and the 'human bomb' incident at Coshquin, County Derry in October 1990, the spring and summer of 1972 saw the greatest concentration of death and destruction from both sides of all the years of the 'troubles'. The IRA bombing campaign was redoubled and there were frequent attacks on the security forces including the Ulster Defence Regiment (UDR), which had replaced the B-Specials and was regarded with some justice as having the same personnel and the same partisan tenor. Protestant private armies were active, the proscribed UVF being joined by the Ulster Defence Association (UDA) which, founded in September 1971, became one of the longer lasting of many acronymically-known groups that were formed with great prodigality during the period and which on the whole had no great record of survival.

The IRA's targets were formally members of the 'occupying

forces' but this rather elastic definition could include civil servants, judges, members of firms that 'worked for' the security forces and even typists. Since Protestant families in rural areas had often contributed members to the UDR, legitimate targets in the eyes of the Provos, the deaths of many young men in areas like west Tyrone were described in retrospect by the Balkan term 'ethnic cleansing'. This seemed to Protestant gangs to confer 'legitimacy' on *their* random killing of Catholics, and indeed this 'terror' response was characteristic of Protestant extremists right into the 1990s, with murderous attacks on a bookmaker's shop in Belfast (February 1992) and public houses in County Derry (October 1993) and County Down (June 1994). There were also several splinter groups on the republican side, notably the Irish National Liberation Army (INLA), which did not base its targets on as precise a description as the IRA.

William Whitelaw, the new 'Northern Ireland supremo', as the papers described him, was an experienced politician with a genius for conciliation, a far cry from Reginald Maudling, Home Secretary in 1970, who is remembered for the phrases: 'an acceptable level of violence' and 'What a bloody awful country!' He began to lay plans for a power-sharing executive led by Faulkner's Unionists and the SDLP. He was assisted in this by the disappointment felt when a promising short-term IRA ceasefire which collapsed in recrimination on 9 July 1972 was followed by general revulsion at 'Bloody Friday' (21 July) when nineteen civilians were killed in a series of twenty-two Provo explosions. The slow decrease in violence after Bloody Friday helped the formation of a new Northern Ireland assembly in which the required moderate majority was secured. Faulkner headed what was for its short life the 'power-sharing executive' with Gerry Fitt of the SDLP as his deputy. The composition of the new administration was hammered out at Sunningdale in Berkshire and represented a triumph for Whitelaw. He manifested an unusual understanding of the situation which he combined with a geniality even more reassuring than James Callaghan's avuncularity had been in 1969.

The first sign that this possibility of lasting peace was doomed like so many others was the return at the 1974 Westminster election of a Labour government, always anathema to Unionists, and the election in Northern Ireland of eleven anti-Faulknerites out of twelve constituencies. The opposition was not so much to power-sharing as to the proposed Council of Ireland, which was seen as a back door to reunification. A general strike was declared on 14 May by the Ulster Workers' Council and 'solidarity' was imposed. The handling of the strike by Harold Wilson and his Secretary of State, Merlyn Rees, left a lot to be desired. The army's role was crucial since it might have been able to maintain essential services, the only significant element in the strike. The army had been ordered out to man these but had been withdrawn, except for the commandeering of petrol dumps for its own needs. Wilson's description of Ulster people as 'spongers' did not help. Faulkner resigned on 28 May and the promising experiment was at an end. At times during the fourteen days of the UWC strike, the terror of civil war, what later commentators have learned to call

'Balkan', seemed to loom, but the most serious occurrences were in Dublin where car bombs killed twenty-five people, and Monaghan where the death toll was six. The perpetrators of these crimes have remained unapprehended and are the subject of continuous speculation.

The political impasse that followed was to become the most characteristic feature of Northern Ireland for the next twenty years. Successive Secretaries of State produced devolution schemes which were rejected by the SDLP or the Unionists. Roy Mason, who succeeded Rees, had learned much from his colleague's experience and was able to face down a strike in 1977 called by a for-once outmarshalled Ian Paisley. Humphrey Atkins, with Thatcher's characteristic adamantine backing, rode out the IRA hunger strikes in 1980 and 1981 when ten republican prisoners, led by Bobby Sands, died in their protest for 'special status', a category that had been withdrawn by Rees in 1976. The deaths were the culmination of five years of action, including the notorious 'blanket' protest. The handling of the situation by the Conservative administration is hard now to understand except as a foolish further proof of 'Iron Lady'-hood. It generated support for the IRA and its political wing Sinn Féin as nothing had done since 'Bloody Sunday'. The period of the deaths, from 5 May to 20 August, was marked by the most serious civil disturbances since internment and the profligate use by army and police of plastic bullets, the much more lethal replacement for rubber bullets, increased the disaffection. In all sixty-one people, including thirty members of the security forces, died.

In 1982 James Prior, the new secretary, tried an initiative
that he dubbed 'rolling devolution' but the SDLP and Sinn
Féin refused to take their seats and Prior would not permit
another Unionist-dominated assembly. A New Ireland Forum
set up by the Irish government and involving all the main
constitutional non-Unionist parties in the island examined
three options for the region's future: as part of a reunited
Ireland, as part of a confederation, or partaking of a system
of joint authority which would give 'equal validity to the two
traditions in Northern Ireland'. The British reaction was
cool but the third option with its 'two-traditions' formula
formed the basis of the Anglo-Irish Agreement of 15
November 1985, signed by Margaret Thatcher and Garrett
FitzGerald, which was meant to reassure both sides and set
up a useful British-Irish Intergovernmental Conference with
a permanent civil service secretariat. Peter Brooke, who
replaced the respected Tom King in 1989, was one of the
more successful Secretaries of State. In 1990 he introduced
the 'Brooke initiative' to establish inter-party talks. This
process was carried on by his successor, Sir Patrick Mayhew,
from 1992.

Through all this IRA and Protestant paramilitaries
continued their campaigns. The Ulster people (and this
applied to the inhabitants of Monaghan, Cavan and Donegal,
to some extent) got used to checkpoints, delays at border
crossings, body and bag searches in stores, cinemas, stations,
air- and seaports. RUC stations, army barracks and government buildings came to resemble medieval fortresses. Patrols
of armed soldiers and police were largely ignored, except by

young people who were often subject to humiliating and pointless attention. The sickening destruction of the commercial hearts of most northern towns, the so-called economic targets, was borne with remarkable fortitude by both sections of the populace, buoyed up by the conviction that such attacks grew ever more pointless. The Irish interest in America was on the whole won away from imprecision and sentimentality, though such IRA feeding agencies as Noraid continued to flourish. An intermittent bombing campaign in the United Kingdom resulted in some display of good old British grit but also caused the arrests of significant numbers of innocent people, most notably the 'Birmingham Six'. Their cases were the subject of prolonged but eventually successful agitation and ruined the reputation of some police forces. 'Innocent until proved Irish' was more than a good joke. The 'mainland' bombing campaign continued into the 1990s, including a 'no-warning' bomb in Warrington which killed two children.

During the years since the fall of the power-sharing executive the constitutional leader of northern nationalists had been John Hume, who proved himself a strong and universally respected statesman (except among right-wing Unionists, who nevertheless conceded him a grudging approbation). Though the paramilitary activity did not abate in ferocity, the IRA under Northern leadership began to test the waters of constitutionalism. The prime *public* figure in this initiative was Gerry Adams, who had captured West Belfast from Gerry Fitt in 1983 only to lose it to Joe Hendron in 1992. Sinn Féin councillors had been active through most of the 1980s and though they proved gadflies their acceptance of political institutions was given a guarded welcome. In a move bristling with risk Hume initiated talks with Adams in the early months of 1988 and in spite of great criticism from many quarters, including members of his own party, continued to arrange for such discussions to take place at different times over the next five years.

The result of these talks and other British-Irish initiatives was a Joint Declaration on 15 December 1993 by John Major, the British prime minister, and Albert Reynolds, the Irish taoiseach. The declaration made it clear that Britain had no selfish interest in Northern Ireland and that it was the 'right of the Irish people alone, by agreement between the two parts . . . to exercise their right of self-determination . . . ' Hume argued that the only reasons for the campaign of violence had been removed. After an expectant summer the IRA declared 'a complete cessation of military operations' on 30 August 1994. There was some semantic argument about the difference, if any, between the word 'permanent' which the British wanted to be used and the word 'complete' which had been used in the IRA declaration, but a cautious confidence, not unmixed with an initial anger, seemed to possess the northern counties. Slowly the paraphernalia of the long war began to disappear with the opening of minor border roads, the decommissioning of permanent checkpoints and a noticeable diminution of army patrols.

The 'peace process', as it has relentlessly been called, took a firm step forward with the declaration of a Protestant paramilitary ceasefire on 13 October, the emergence of possible political wings in the Ulster Democratic Party and the Progressive Unionist Party, and the appearance on the scene of such spokespersons as Gary McMichael. (Throughout the negotiations Ian Paisley and the DUP were notable for their predictably uncooperative attitude, in distinct contrast to James Molyneaux and the UUP, who maintained a helpful silence.) It was able to withstand the killing of a Post Office worker in a raid in Newry in November by known members of the IRA. Indeed the virtually universal condemnation of the atrocity increased the confidence of a people desensitised after twenty-five years of 'troubles'. The 'first Christmas of peace' was celebrated throughout Ireland, Belfast greeted a remarkable number of shoppers from the Republic and the Northern Ireland Tourist Board reported evidence of a huge interest in Ulster holidays for the coming summer. The first day of the new year, conveniently a Sunday, saw many church services for peace and it was not thought fanciful that thanksgiving prayers and hymns for the first time seemed to outweigh those of supplication. The best touch of all was the welcoming-in of 1995 with an informal meeting of people who lived along the peace line between the Falls and the Shankill.

No one doubted that what had been accomplished so far was the merest of preliminaries, and a region where even the young have an unusual political awareness is unlikely to be starry-eyed about a problem that carries the weight of more than 300 years of troubled history. As these words are being written caution takes primacy over euphoria but there is a palpable delight in peace and a undramatic, unrhetorical determination on the part of ordinary people to maintain it, and to afford a chance of success to the complicated and sensitive political negotiations between Dublin, London and Northern Ireland politicians.

A CHRONOLOGY OF ULSTER HISTORY

30,000 BC	Ulster's topography established
7000–6500 BC	Human habitation at Mount Sandel
2500 BC	Building of passage graves, notably Newgrange
1200 BC	Late bronze-age artefacts
680 BC	Circular habitation enclosure at Emain Macha
AD 1–500	Building of crannogs, hill forts and raths
200	Conn Céd-cathach establishes high kingship of Tara
300–450	Irish raids on Roman Britain
400	Eoghan and Conall, sons of Niall Noígiallach, establish kingdom of Aileach
432	Traditional date of the coming of St Patrick
536	Colum Cille begins his mission to Iona
575	Convention of Druim Cett
664	Synod of Whitby
795	First Viking raids
841	Foundation of permanent Viking colony in Dublin
964	Rise of Dál Cais and beginning of hegemony of Brian Boru
1014	Battle of Clontarf and death of Brian
1095–1148	Reforming activity of St Malachy
1155	Bull *Laudabiliter*
1166	Expulsion of Dermot MacMurrough
1170	Landing of Strongbow
1171	Henry II lands in Ireland
1175	John de Courcy invades Ulster
1315	Edward Bruce lands at Larne
1478-1513	Rule of Garret Mór Fitzgerald
1534	Rebellion of 'Silken Thomas'
1561	Rebellion of Shane O'Neill
1587	Hugh O'Neill proclaimed Earl of Tyrone
1588	Ships of Spanish Armada wrecked on Ulster coast
1595–1603	Nine Years War between O'Neill, O'Donnell and English forces
1598	Battle of the Yellow Ford
1601	O'Neill's defeat at Kinsale
1607	'Flight of the Earls'
1608–10	British colonisation of Ulster
1639	'Black Oath' imposed on Ulster Scots by Wentworth
1641	Outbreak of Ulster rebellion
1642	Owen Roe O'Neill takes command of Irish forces
1646	Battle of Benburb

1649	Cromwell arrives in Ireland. Massacres at Drogheda, Wexford. Premature death of Owen Roe
1652	Act for the Settling of Ireland
1653	Forfeiture of Irish lands and transplantation
1679	Arrest of Oliver Plunkett (executed 1681)
1687	Tyrconnell Lord Deputy
1688	Closing of the gates of Derry
1689	Siege of Derry lifted
1690	Battle of Boyne
1691	Treaty of Limerick
1695	Penal laws
1704	Further penal laws (Queen Anne's reign)
1760	Thurot lands French force at Carrickfergus
1782	Dungannon convention of Volunteers
1791	Foundation of United Irishmen in Belfast
1795	'Battle of the Diamond' at Loughgall, County Armagh leads to founding of Orange Order
1798	Rebellion breaks out in Wexford, Antrim and Down. McCracken and other leaders hanged. Tone, captured in Lough Swilly, commits suicide
1800	Act of Union
1841	Daniel O'Connell visits Belfast
1842	Charles Gavan Duffy becomes editor of *Nation*, organ of Young Ireland movement
1845–8	Famine caused by potato blight. Western and southern counties of Ulster mainly affected
1845	Queen's College founded in Belfast
1857	Serious sectarian disturbances in Belfast
1861	Derryveagh evictions
1862	Shipbuilding firm of Harland and Wolff founded
1865	Magee College, Derry founded
1877	J. G. Biggar devises 'obstructive' tactics for Irish Parliamentary party
1886	Lord Randolph Churchill's anti-Home Rule visit to Belfast
1893	Eoin MacNeill helps found the Gaelic League
1905	Formation of Ulster Unionist Council and pro-Home Rule Dungannon Club (by Bulmer Hobson)
1910	Carson becomes leader of Irish Unionists
1912	Solemn League and Covenant
1913	Foundation of Ulster Volunteer Force
1914	Curragh 'Mutiny'; UVF gun-running; Home Rule Bill becomes law but shelved till end of war (from 4 August)
1916	Easter rising; Unionists agree to a partitioned Ulster

1920	Sectarian riots in Belfast and Derry; formation of Ulster Special Constabulary begins; Ulster partitioned under Government of Ireland Act, Sir James Craig prime minister
1922	Special Powers Act (made permanent 1933)
1925	After failure of Boundary Commission existing border accepted
1943	Sir Basil Brooke becomes prime minister of Northern Ireland
1949	Guarantee by Britain of Northern Ireland's remaining part of UK at its parliament's discretion
1956–62	Operation Harvest – IRA's border campaign
1963	Terence O'Neill becomes PM of Northern Ireland
1965	Sean Lemass and O'Neill meet at Stormont. Opposition by Ian Paisley
1968	Police clash with NICRA marchers in Derry followed by severe rioting
1969	People's Democracy march attacked at Burntollet. After a spring and summer of rioting and growing tension army called out to keep peace in Derry and after anti-Catholic disturbances in Belfast
1971	Start of Provisional IRA's campaign. Lasts till 1994. Answered by intermittent Protestant terrorist activity
1971	Continuing IRA campaign leads to internment
1972	Thirteen anti-internment demonstrators killed in Derry. Stormont prorogued
1973	Sunningdale agreement leads to formation of power-sharing executive
1974	Executive brought down by UWC general strike
1976	'Peace People' movement
1977	Brian Faulkner, last prime minister of Northern Ireland, dies in hunting accident
1981	Ten hunger strikers die in 'special category' campaign. Severe violence and increase in following of IRA
1985	Anglo-Irish Agreement between Margaret Thatcher and Garret FitzGerald
1987	Remembrance Day bomb in Enniskillen kills eleven people
1988	Talks between Gerry Adams of Sinn Féin and John Hume of SDLP
1993	Downing Street Declaration signed by John Major and Albert Reynolds as a result of many secret talks
1994	IRA ceasefire; Protestant paramilitary ceasefire

SELECT BIBLIOGRAPHY

Adamnán. *Vita Columbae* (ed. W Reeves). Dublin, 1857.

Adamson, I. *The Cruthin.* Bangor, 1974.

——————, *The Identity of Ulster.* Belfast, 1982.

Akenson, D. H. *The Irish Education Experiment: The National System of Education in the Nineteenth Century.* London, 1970.

Arthur, P. and K. Jeffery. *Northern Ireland since 1968.* Oxford, 1988.

Bardon, J. *A History of Ulster.* Belfast, 1992.

Barrington, J. *The Rise and Fall of the Irish Nation.* Paris, 1833.

Bartlett, T. and D. Hayton (eds.). *Penal Era and Golden Age: Essays in Irish History 1690–1800.* Belfast, 1979.

Beckett, J. C. *The Making of Modern Ireland 1603–1923.* London, 1966.

Bew, P. *Conflict and Conciliation in Ireland 1890–1910.* Oxford, 1987.

Blake, J. W. *Northern Ireland in the Second World War.* Belfast, 1956.

Brady, C. and R. Gillespie. *Natives and Newcomers; the Making of Irish Colonial Society 1534–1641.* Dublin, 1986.

Buckland, P. *Irish Unionism* Vol I: *The Anglo-Irish and the New Ireland 1885–1922.* Vol II: *Ulster Unionism and the Origins of Northern Ireland 1886–1922.* Dublin, 1973.

——————, *The Factory of Grievances: Devolved Government in Northern Ireland 1921–39.* Dublin, 1979.

Chadwick, N. *The Celts.* London, 1970.

Collins, P. (ed.). *Nationalism and Unionism: Conflict in Ireland 1885–1921.* Belfast, 1994.

Connolly, S. *Priests and People in Pre-Famine Ireland 1780–1845.* Dublin, 1982.

Coogan, T. P. *The IRA.* London, 1980.

Corish, P. J. The *Catholic Community in the Seventeenth and Eighteenth Centuries.* Dublin, 1981.

Crawford, W. H. and B. Trainor (eds.). *Aspects of Irish Social History 1750–1800.* Belfast, 1969.

Curtis, E. *A History of Ireland.* London, 1936.

de Paor, L. *Divided Ulster.* London, 1970.

Dickson, R. H. *Ulster Emigration to Colonial America 1718–1785.* Belfast, 1966.

Doyle, D. N. *Ireland, Irishmen and Revolutionary America 1760–1820.* Dublin, 1981.

Edwards R. D. and T. D. Williams. *The Great Famine.* London, 1956 (Reprinted: Dublin, 1994).

Elliott, E. *Partners in Revolution: The United Irishmen and France.* London, 1982.

Farrell, M. *Northern Ireland: the Orange State.* London, 1976.

Fisk, R. *In Time of War: Ireland, Ulster and the Price of Neutrality 1939–1945*. London, 1983.

Foster, R. F. *Modern Ireland 1600– 1972*. London, 1988.

Gray, J. *City in Revolt: James Larkin and the Belfast Dock Strike of 1907*. Belfast, 1985.

Harkness, D W. *Northern Ireland since 1920*. Dublin, 1983.

Johnston, E. M. *Great Britain and Ireland 1760–1800*. Edinburgh, 1963.

Kennedy, L. and P. Ollerenshaw (eds.). *An Economic History of Ulster 1820–1940*. Manchester, 1985.

Lacy, B. *Siege City. The Story of Derry and Londonderry*. Belfast, 1990.

Lee, J. *Ireland 1912–1985, Politics and Society*. Cambridge, 1989.
————, *The Modernisation of Irish Society 1848–1918*. Dublin, 1973.

Lyons, F. S. L. *Ireland since the Famine*. London, 1971.

McCann, E. *War and an Irish Town*. London, 1974.

Mac Airt, S. and G. Mac Niocaill (eds.). *Annála Uladh*. Dublin, 1983.

Mac Niocaill, G. *Ireland before the Vikings*. Dublin, 1972.

Mallory, J. P. and T. E. McNeill. *The Archaeology of Ulster*. Belfast, 1991.

Miller, D. *Queen's Rebels: Ulster Loyalism in Historical Perspective*. Dublin, 1978.

Moody, T. W. *The Londonderry Plantation 1609–1641*. Belfast, 1939.

Moody. T. W. and F. X. Martin (eds.). *The Course of Irish History*. Cork, 1994 (3rd ed.).

Murphy, D. *Derry, Donegal and Modern Ulster 1790–1921*. Derry, 1981.

O'Connor, F. *In Search of a State*. Belfast, 1993.

Patterson, H. *Class Conflict and Sectarianism; The Protestant Working Class and the Belfast Labour Movement 1868–1920*. Belfast, 1980.

Raftery, J. et al. *The Celts*. Cork, 1964.

Roebuck, P. (ed.). *Plantation to Partition*. Belfast, 1981.

Rumpf, E. and A. C. Hepburn. *Nationalism and Socialism in Twentieth-Century Ireland*. Liverpool, 1977.

Senior, H. *Orangeism in Ireland and Britain 1795–1836*. London, 1960.

Simms, J. G. *Jacobite Ireland 1685–1691*. London, 1969.
————, *The Siege of Derry*. Dublin, 1966.

Stewart, A. T. Q. *The Narrow Ground, Aspects of Ulster 1609–1969*. London, 1977.
————, *The Ulster Crisis*. London, 1967.

Townshend, C. *Political Violence in Ireland: Government and Resistance since 1848*. Oxford, 1983.

Walker, B. *Ulster Politics: The Formative Years 1869–86*. Belfast 1989.

Walsh, J. R. and T. Bradley. *A History of the Irish Church 400–700*. Dublin, 1991.

Whyte, J. *Church and State in Modern Ireland 1923–1979*. London, 1980.

Young, A. *A Tour of Ireland 1776–1779*. London, 1892.

INDEX

Gladstone, W.E., 112, 128, 130, 131-4, 138, 144
Glenarm, Co. Antrim, 134
Glenveagh, Co. Donegal, 129
Good, James Winder, 125
Gormflaith, 38
Gough, General, 140
Government of Ireland Act, 1920, 144-5
Government of Ireland Bill, 1886, 132-3
'graces', 74
Grattan, Henry, 47, 102, 104, 105, 109
Great Famine, 117-19
Great Northern, 125
Gregory, Lady, 38, 93, 134-5
Grey, Lord, 50
Griffith, Arthur, 136, 141, 143
Grocers, company of, 70
gun-runnings, 140
Gunpowder Plot, 58

Hacketts, 44
Hamilton, James, 62
Hamilton, Richard, 85, 86, 87
Hannay, Canon James O., 126
Hanoverians, 102
Harland and Wolff, 124, 142
Harold, King, 30
Hasting, Battle of, 30
Heath, Edward, 169
Hendron, Joe, 179
Henry, Paul, 125
Henry, Robert M., 125
Henry I, 39
Henry II, 39-40
Henry V, 41
Henry VII, 43, 46-7, 49
Henry VIII, 43, 49-52
Hervey, Frederick, Earl Bishop of Derry, 99
Hibernia, 10
Hobson, Bulmer, 125, 136, 139, 141
Hogg and McIntyre, 123
Hogg and Mitchell, 123

Home Rule, 121, 124, 125, 130, 136
and unionists, 131-4, 137-40
Hope, Jemmy, 105
housing, 152, 160-1, 166
Housing Trust, 160-1
Humbert, General Jean, 108
Hume, John, 168, 178-9
Hundred Years War, 43
hunger strikes, 173, 176
Hyde, Douglas, 134-5

Imbolc, 28
Inch, 44
industrial revolution, 98-9, 121-7
Inishmore, Aran Islands, 26
Inishowen, Co. Donegal, 19, 45, 47, 59, 62, 68, 99
Innocent XI, Pope, 83
internment, 171
Iona, 26, 27, 32-3
Ireton, General, 77
Irish Free State, 148, 151
Irish language, 9, 14, 48, 159, 162
revival, 134
18th century, 100
in Ulster, 135
Irish National Liberation Army (INLA), 174
Irish National Theatre, 93, 136
Irish parliamentary party, 125, 131-2, 136, 150
Irish Rebellion, The (Temple), 77
Irish Republican Army (IRA), 143-4, 145, 146, 157, 162-3, 168, 170, 173-4, 176, 178
ceasefire, 179
Irish Republican Brotherhood (IRB), 125, 128, 136
Irish Society, 69-70, 79
Irish Volunteers, 139, 141
Iron Age, 12, 16
Islandmagee, 77
Ita of Kileedy, St, 28
Ivar of Limerick, 35-6

O'More, Rory, 89
O'More, Sir Rory, 75
O'Mores, 47
O'Neill, Conn Bacach, 51, 52, 54
O'Neill, Hugh, 7, 48
O'Neill, Hugh, Earl of Tyrone, 54-60, 61, 67, 75
O'Neill, Niall, 47
O'Neill, Owen Roe, 75-6
O'Neill, Sir Phelim, 75
O'Neill, Shane (the Proud), 52-4
O'Neill, Terence, 163-4, 165-6, 168
O'Neills, 19, 46, 47-8, 51
Orange Order, 107, 109, 124, 129
  banned, 114-15
  founded, 97, 106
  marches, 153-4, 159
O'Reillys, 46, 53
Ormond, Earl of, 75, 76, 79
Ormonds, 46
O'Rourke, Tiernán, 38-9
Orr, William, 107
Ota, 33
O'Toole, St Laurence, 42

Paine, Tom, 104
Paisley, Ian, 164-5, 170, 176, 180
Pale, the, 43, 51, 53, 54
parliament, Irish, 47, 102-4, 109
parliament, Northern Ireland. see Stormont
Parnell, Charles S., 125, 128, 131, 134, 136, 144
Partholón, 14
partition, 123, 124, 143, 144
Party Processions Act, 115
Patrick, St, 22-5
Patriotic Parliament, 84-5
Paulett, George, 67
peace process, 179-81
Pearse, Patrick, 139
peat, 98
Peep o'Day Boys, 106

penal laws, 93, 95-7
Penitentials (Patrick), 24
People's Democracy, 166, 168
Peronne, 28
Perrott, Deputy, 57
Philip II, of Spain, 52
Philip III, of Spain, 56, 57, 59
Picts, 16, 25
Pirrie, William, 124, 142
Pitt, William, 105, 109, 112
Pius X, Pope, 137
plantations, 51, 52, 91
Plunkett, St Oliver, 79
poets, 14, 18
Pontis, M., 86
Popish Plot, 79
population, 91
Portadown, Co. Armagh, 77
Portrush, Co. Antrim, 32, 44
potato, 98
Poynings' Law, 47, 85, 103
Presbyterians, 64, 66, 73, 74, 76, 87, 91, 100
  attitude to Catholics, 96-7
  education, 149-50
  emigration, 94-5
  and Home Rule, 125-6
  legal disabilities, 96
  numbers of, 116
  Test Acts, 94
  and unionism, 111-12
  United Irishmen, 104-5
Prior, James, 177
Pritani, 16
Progressive Unionist Party, 180
proportional representation, 145
Protestant Telegraph, 165
Protestants, 83, 90
  attitude to Catholics, 110-11, 115-16
  emigration, 116, 119-20
  in Gaelic League, 135
  Protestant nation, 91-101
  separatist movement, 102-9
  unionism, 111-12
Provisional IRA, 169, 170-1
  targets of, 173-4

201

Donegal

Derry

Derry

Antrim

Belfast

Tyrone

Fermanagh

Armagh

Down

Monaghan

Cavan

- - - - - Province boundaries

———— Boundary between Republic
and Northern Ireland